# PRAISE FOR KNOW YOURSELF

"At a time of wounded bodies and spirits, of emotional and social ills, and of turmoil and loss, how does one find inner strength and peace? Know Yourself offers to people of all backgrounds a needed answer to this question. In her intellectually rich and deeply moving personal meditation on finding, knowing, and becoming a person of compassion, Lexie Potamkin provides an array of philosophical and spiritual pathways to a better, more meaningful life. Most of all, she blesses us with insights that help us to be true to ourselves through embracing a self-love capacious enough to love those who are different from us."

*— Evelyn Brooks Higginbotham, PhD, Professor of History and of African and African American Studies, Harvard University*

"In *Know Yourself*, Lexie Brockway Potamkin offers rich insight for self-awareness and discovery, winding through spiritual philosophy, wise teachings, and meditative experience. Though the pathway may be new, readers will instinctively feel they are not alone as she not only invites but accompanies and guides us throughout the journey inward - with her wisdom, warmth, and sense of wonder."

*— Gail J. Stearns, Dean of the Wallace All Faiths Chapel, Chapman University*

"Lexie Brockway Potamkin is a generous and beautiful soul who has been a devoted supporter of the work of His Holiness the Dalai Lama and of our work at Emory University and Drepung Loseling Monastery. She has long been committed to her own spiritual practice and to learning all she could about how to make the world a more compassionate place. Her years of experience, and her loving heart, are clear in this thoughtful and inspiring book."

*— Lobsang Tenzin Negi, PhD, Professor of Pedagogy, Department of Religion Executive Director, Center for Contemplative Science and Compassion-Based Ethics Emory University*

"Lexie has spent years immersed in the work of bringing more compassion to our world. It's a wonderful thing for us all that she has shared her journey while creating a brilliant roadmap from it for achieving true happiness. This is an incredibly soul-nurturing book that is exactly what the world needs right now."

— *Marco Borges, New York Times best-selling author, exercise physiologist and founder & CEO of 22 Days Nutrition*

"In her book, *Know Yourself*, Lexie guides the reader through a journey of transformation. A devoted meditator, Lexie explores new ground by merging meditation, psychology, and philosophy... inspiring you towards transcendence... Revealing her own personal journey, Lexie teaches you how to focus and calm your mind to hear your own inner voice, and discover your true vocation. Lexie is the perfect example of a self-actualized, authentic, and compassionate person. Her magnetic warmth informs all who know her that within her friendship can be found a safe harbor. *Know Yourself* is a must-read for everyone who is searching for a contemporary approach to ancient wisdom. By teaching the importance of the interior life, and by living the interior life, Lexie charts the course towards personal transitions. Lexie and I have been friends for over thirty-five years and I can honestly say that *Know Yourself* is the exquisite testament to her beautiful soul."

— *Dr. Gail Gross, PhD, EdD, MEd, nationally recognized family, child development, and human behavior expert and author of The Only Way Out is Through and How to Build Your Baby's Brain*

"*Know Yourself* speaks to the very soul of a wounded world coping in the midst of crises and to the heart of humanity seeking hope for a brighter future. Lexie's valuable lessons for achieving both personal transformation and global peace guide us to explore the fundamental nature of our core identity, purpose in life, and sense of being. Integrating timeless spiritual truths, cutting-edge science, and her own personal wisdom, *Know Yourself* provides the timely antidote we require to become a happier, stronger, and more compassionate world."

— Dr. Jay Kumar, Author of *Science of a Happy Brain*

"Lexie Potamkin has written this wonderful book to aid the reader to have a more meaningful participation in daily living."

— *Richard A. Sprague, legendary Philadelphia trial lawyer and founder of Sprague & Sprague*

"Lexie has written a book filled with easy-to-use tools and techniques to help bring people more balance and peace of mind. In a world filled with so much suffering, her book, *Know Yourself*, offers a ray of hope that through compassion for ourselves and others we can make our world a better place."

— *Dr. Brigitt Rok, Clinical Psychologist.*

"Lexie Brockway Potamkin has long been on a quest for self-awareness. Through her many books, I along with many others have joined her on that quest. Her latest book, *Know Yourself*, took me on a journey that opened my mind so that I could see life through a more compassionate lens. Getting caught up in this compelling book reminded me what it's like to learn from a wise and knowing teacher."

— *James L. Doti, President Emeritus and Professor of Economics, Chapman University*

# KNOW
## YOURSELF

# KNOW
# YOURSELF

## DEVELOP A MORE COMPASSIONATE, STRONGER, AND HAPPIER YOU

### LEXIE BROCKWAY POTAMKIN

Publisher: What is Peace, LLC

Editor: Laurie Sue Brockway

Cover Design and Interior: Qamber Designs & Media

Cover image of tree: V.G./DepositPhotos.com

Photos: Lexie Brockway Potamkin images with spiritual figures were taken with permission and are part of the author's personal photo collection.

All other images are used under license from: Shutterstock.com and DepositPhotos.com

Print Edition ISBN: 978-0-9824590-4-1

Every effort has been made to ensure the accuracy of this book. It has been reviewed by multiple copyeditors and proofreaders, as well as experts in Buddhism, psychology, and religion. It was edited as closely as possible in accordance with the *Chicago Manual of Style*, 17th Edition. Some words and names are from the Pali, Sanskrit, or other traditions, and may have different spellings in each, with accents in different places. We removed the accents throughout the text to avoid confusion and we capitalized certain divine references out of respect.

Much of this book reflects the author's experiences and memories, and her interpretation of various philosophies based on her many years of spiritual research and meditation practice. The information is shared in the spirit of educational purposes. This is meant to be a transformative work in that it adds or extends the existing knowledge base. It contains philosophical, cultural, and spiritual concepts from a wide variety of sources for the purpose of informing and inspiring readers. Many of the classic quotes, poems, prayers and epigraphs from various philosophies have been used so widely that they are part of the culture; we identify the author, creator, and source wherever possible. Wisdom of the Buddha and His Holiness the Dalai Lama are ingrained in the everyday practices of Buddhism and are used herein in the spirit of inspiring readers to understand the power of compassion. Attributions for all sources can be found in the extensive Chapter Notes section and Bibliography. Please purchase only authorized editions.

Author's Note: I'd like to thank my long-time friend and associate, Rev. Laurie Sue Brockway, for her editorial guidance and insights, and her husband, Rev. Dr. Victor Fuhrman, for joining the team to help with research and proofreading.

I dedicate this book to my family and friends.
They guide and sustain me and make this world a
brighter place.
And to my spiritual family and wisdom teachers,
I thank you for all you have given and shared.
Through your generous teachings,
and through many sacred interactions,
I have learned so much.
May the blessings given to me be passed along
now to those who read these pages.

# CONTENTS

# FOREWORD

*"Knowing yourself is the beginning of all wisdom."*
— *Aristotle*

*Know Yourself: Develop a More Compassionate, Stronger, and Happier You* is a true testament to the gift of being human! And Lexie Brockway Potamkin is a true gift to all that know her personally and get to meet her within her books. It is an honor to introduce readers to her latest, inspiring book because it is filled with so many ways to make our lives better and brighter, arriving precisely at a time when our world needs the rays of hope that shine so brightly throughout these pages.

This book is a personal guide on how to go deep within, find our truest nature, and how to expand outward with love and compassion. Within our hearts, spirits, minds, and bodies lie our greatest wisdom and treasures, some already present in our lives, and others awaiting to be revealed. Lexie generously offers us a blueprint for discovering our gifts, treasures, meaning and purpose, while learning to discover our 'Endless Knot' of interdependence and connection.

Lexie is not only an ever-seeking student of life and its many wonders, but she is also a humble and ever-giving healer, sage and teacher. You will get to meet Lexie firsthand, and experience her compassionate heart and gentle, guiding spirit as she walks with us through understanding life philosophies, cultures, psychological impacts on personality and personal development, her own plights of dealing with suffering, loss, and change, and how Buddhist wisdom teachings have offered a pathway into our sacred self.

It often takes a journey through the darkness and pain of grief and loss to turn one into a great healer. This is a journey I know Lexie immersed herself in because I took it with her, when we taught a Meaning-Centered Grief workshop exploring our own griefs and becoming reconnected to Meaning in Life even amidst our losses; and when we supported one another through the loss of our mutual, dear friend. But even before that, Lexie picked up the pieces of her broken heart after losing her father at a young and impressionable age, and then again, after losing her mother. It set her on a path of learning to embrace grief and all its difficult and bitter-sweet lessons. And it led her to reach out her gentle hand to help others through her teachings, online courses, and books. In the process of walking through the terrains of grief, Lexie discovered the true lessons of impermanence and was able to embrace a concept that is so difficult for most of us—that everything changes. The inevitability of change and building our capacity to accept it with openness and comfort is one of the many important messages in this book. The "how" to accept change is the hard part, but Lexie teaches us the methods and tools for taking on this most valuable undertaking, and embracing it collectively.

Lexie and I have also taught workshops on Transforming Relationships together. As part of our ever-evolving change process, transformation is our ability and capability; and something we can learn to cultivate in order to create more dynamic and sustainable connections to self and others. Lexie's genuine love and kindness for humanity, smiling heart and authenticity are offered to every person she meets, and within these pages. Transforming our relationship with ourselves, including honoring and loving ourselves, as well as having all the love we deserve in our relationships with others, is Lexie's ultimate wish for all of us. This is another important message that permeates throughout this book.

Creating bridges of connection between science and psychology with spiritual practice and faith traditions, *Know Yourself* celebrates and welcomes ancient guidance with present-day techniques, all centered through and around compassion. Throughout the insightful story-telling, coupled with current scientific research, Lexie offers practical ways to learn how to meditate, relax our bodies, center our attention and energy, and cultivate our own wisdom tool kit.

All pathways explored within these pages, with its easy-to-do exercises along the way, lead toward the sacred space of discovering the meaning inherent in life and our ultimate connectedness on our journey. This is a book you will keep on your night table and in your daily bag, to help keep you grounded throughout your days and evenings.

As an integrative psychologist, and a mind-body-spirit teacher and practitioner, I highly recommend this compassion-infused book for everyone looking for more balance, contentment, understanding, presence-practice, and overall lasting happiness. I am very passionate about sharing it with my fellow journeyers in my personal and professional life, because I know it will have a tremendously positive impact on all who read it, and that it offers enduring tools and techniques for our ongoing personal growth and transformation. May your journey through *Know Yourself* help you discover your Sacred Compassionate Self.

Marie S. Dezelic, PhD, PsyD
Author of *Meaning-Centered Therapy Workbook*
*Meaning-Centered Therapy Manual*
*Trauma Treatment: Healing the Whole Person*
*Transcending Grief*
*Transforming Relationships*

# INTRODUCTION

# You Have the Power to Know Yourself and Transform Yourself

*"What is necessary to change a person is to change their awareness of themselves."*
*— Abraham Maslow*

I USED TO BE A TYPE-A business owner, ensconced in corporate America. Over the last twenty-two years, I've tried to help others as a human rights activist, minister, and philanthropist, and by creating web content and books that inspire others. My parents always taught me that a smile is one of our most valuable assets—it is free and easy to do—so I have tried to bring a smile, and perhaps inspire one, wherever possible.

My curiosity, my own upbringing, and ultimately the loss of my parents led me to write about some of the qualities and experiences in life that seemed important and universal. After interviewing thousands of people, I discovered that even the topics that impact most humans are often seen and experienced through a different lens for each person. I published a series of five books that I considered to be "messages from the heart." They are: *What Is Spirit, What Is Peace, What Is Love, What Is Death,* and *What Is Laughter?*

As thousands of people from all walks of life shared their views, I came to understand that everyone carried a certain belief or point of view that was derived from their own personal philosophy on life. And in each of my books, people took the time to sit with me for an interview and to think about these topics—

Spirit, Peace, Love, Death, and Laughter—and offer thoughtful answers from the heart.

Having been privy to people's innermost thoughts and generous sharing, it was uplifting for me as the author and for the interviewees of my books to engage in these kinds of conversations. It was sometimes transformational because there was an open and honest dialogue that offered a way for both of us to share in a meaningful exploration. From former President Jimmy Carter to the waitress at a favorite restaurant, from top business executives, astronauts, school teachers, and new moms, I learned so much from everyone who shared their thoughts.

I've also learned so much from my family over these years. Nurturing a long-term marriage of thirty-five years and raising children has obviously given me a whole new perspective on life and also reminded me of (and helped me fine-tune) my own personal philosophy.

We all know the saying, "I opened my mouth ... and my mother came out." That is definitely true, because the values we were raised with from our own parents are the foundation of what we impart to our kids. They seep into life unconsciously and automatically for most of us. But I found child-rearing highlighted my true values and principles again and again, and made me more aware of the beliefs that made me who I was.

Raising kids is hectic, and we all know that our beloved offspring develop their own minds and ways of doing things as they grow—this is how it is meant to be. As my kids were growing up, I realized it was even more important for me to continue my own inner journey. As my meditation and spirituality practices progressed, I found myself thinking about a new book, a book in which I could share insights about one of the most important things I have learned: compassion. I thought the best way to do this was to share my own journey and to describe the fascinating and evolutionary pathways that led me to a more meaningful life.

That's how *Know Yourself: Develop a More Compassionate,*

*Stronger, and Happier You* was born, as a way to help others onto a path of true happiness. I hope it puts a smile on your face, or at least gets you thinking about things with an open mind.

Just as the people featured in my other books were from all walks of life, this book is meant for readers from all backgrounds. My intention is that anyone, of any age, can find some value in these pages.

There are so many people who have touched my life—too many to enumerate, but I am eternally grateful to each. They have shared their wisdom generously and have each added a building block to my understanding of the things I explore in these pages. But there is one person I want to mention, because he died and left me a truly meaningful parting gift. His name is Dr. *Robert* D. *Willix,* Jr., MD, a former cardiac surgeon who was a pioneer in energy medicine and a very wise soul. He called me a few days before he died and, in the midst of writing this book, he reminded me of *my own* awakening to self-awareness.

One day, years ago, we were meditating together and he turned to me with a message that changed my life. He said: "Look, you came into this world meant to be a healer, a meditator, a very reflective kind of person who goes inward and does inner work. But what happened is your dad died when you were nineteen, and you became this Type-A personality. You had to be successful and work hard. You had to help with your mom. You felt compelled to work, work, work, and do, do, do, because your dad died. You were compensating for his loss and maybe trying to deflect the pain."

He paused, and added: "But it's really not who you are, and you need to know yourself. You're really not a Type-A person, and it would really do you well if you meditated more."

I can still remember the tears that came down my face because it really struck a chord of truth for me.

Being in touch with him again was such a strong reminder of the things he taught me over the course of our friendship. He encouraged me to see myself for who I truly am, and embrace myself. He inspired me to identify my true personal philosophy as well as the kinds of experiences that made me feel like I was home. And so I did.

I discovered that I love spending time with my dear friends, family, and the Tibetan Buddhist monks I have long been affiliated with—you will learn more about them later! I recognized that being with other loving, compassionate people makes me feel happy and that exploring new traditions uplifts me. I began to nurture my *real* personality and to do things that fed my soul.

I'd spent years in the business world operating from the Type-A personality, and I am grateful for the lessons and the experiences that shaped me and helped me grow. Work is my tonic and I love being productive, but it was my dear friend Bob who pointed out that I had trained myself to go against my own nature and showed me how I had overridden who I am. I needed balance in my life.

I credit him with helping me get in touch with and acknowledge my true spirit. He listened compassionately as I shared my truth: I was born on a farm in Idaho. I used to play with imaginary fairies. I was the youngest child. I was alone a lot. I communed with nature. I felt at peace being out in nature. I remember riding horses and being out all day playing in the woods by myself and picking flowers. And I came into this life with this wonderful, gentle, calm, peaceful childhood. Then my father died when I was still a teen and I became a workaholic, living in New York City.

There must be others who have lost sight of their true selves and may not even be aware of what drives them each day.

Bob's call brought it all back to me and confirmed it was time to finish this book so that others may gain insights from what I have learned from many of the wonderful teachers and inspiring people who have crossed my path.

In my own journey, I have discovered that when you are open-minded you find great teachers are *everywhere*. They may not be typical teachers or gurus; in fact, your teachers may be your kids, your sage hair stylist, or a precious friend who always imparts just what you need to hear. As time goes on, we learn to be our own great teachers, and as we fill up with wisdom we can also teach others.

My hope for all who hold this book in their hands is that you discover that the greatest teacher lives in your own heart and mind and that you have a personal well of insight. That's why *discovering* the truth of your own mind and heart is essential.

## What You'll Find in These Pages

This is not a book that insists you adopt a particular philosophy or spiritual approach. It is more of a guide to help you reach a greater state of self-awareness so that you can assess the beliefs that drive and inspire you—and add in some new ones you might discover along the way. Perhaps most importantly, it is hoped you can become more compassionate toward yourself and that this will extend to others.

I have not lost my connection to the messages of the heart that others so graciously shared with me in my earlier books, but this book will focus more on cultivating an open mind and inspiring curiosity. You will learn some of my favorite approaches to a happier, more compassionate life, including the Four Virtues of the Heart from the Buddhist tradition. This book combines modern practices, ancient philosophies, mindfulness, meditation, and psychology.

Most importantly, it will show new ways to focus our awareness, tame our minds, and find peace, calm, and happiness—even in difficult times.

PART ONE. Learn about how our personal philosophies develop and live, as well as how we can expand our view by considering insights from different cultures. I will share ways in which I learned to embrace all people and how it led me on a search for traditions steeped in compassion.

**PART TWO.** Take a journey through Buddhism, a tradition close to my heart. I'll share all the best parts of my experience as well as revealing the sacred wisdom that has empowered my life in so many ways. The teachings in these chapters include the Buddhist approach to peace of mind, an open heart, and a happy compassionate life. You can put these ideas into action immediately. There are many things to learn on this topic, but it is just one philosophy that offers us a new way of looking at the world.

**PART THREE.** Dive more deeply into some other favorite world traditions. Take a trip to the Temple of Apollo, learn about Pluralism and Relativism, discover the ancient history of Indian philosophies, and learn about the gentle power of the Tao.

**PART FOUR.** I share my tips on how to meditate, as well as offering some of the most powerful meditations and exercises I know.

**PART FIVE.** Learn how to feed your body, mind, and spirit at the same time and discover how to become a Beautiful Hero.

I am a minister, but this book is not meant to preach a certain belief or way of life. I consider this a call to action for the soul. Your soul. We live in an age filled with distractions that prevent us from our own personal growth and that influence our views and life philosophy, and not always in a positive way. In the overwhelming nature of life's daily duties, we surrender to the path of least resistance, and sometimes we even seek out others to help us formulate our point of view. Or it could be that we choose to have no particular belief about life, and this can lead us to become aimless or unhappy.

My deepest hope is that this book may be of use to you in finding your happiness, fulfillment, and true meaning in your life; that you come to understand the personal philosophy that has carried you through life, and maybe make some new choices about your approach to life.

With All My Blessings,
Lexie

# LET'S BEGIN: TAKE A MOMENT TO MEDITATE

I invite you to begin this book with a brief meditation. Meditation is a way to expand awareness and also to ground oneself. When I use the word "ground" or "grounding," it means a form of centering and calming. When you ground yourself during meditation, it may mean putting two feet on the ground—terra firma—so that you feel secure and stable. That makes it easier to allow your mind to go into a meditative process.

Try this meditation. I have found it very useful, and I hope you do too.

Take a moment for you, because you are worth it.

- Start by relaxing your muscles in your face. Allow your mind to settle into silence and close your eyes.
- Focus on your breath and ask yourself: Who am I? Beyond the roles that I play every day, who am I really? Who am I?
- And now, silently ask yourself: What do I want? Beyond my necessities, what do I *really* want? What do I really want?
- Now ask yourself: What is my purpose? What are my gifts that I have to heal myself and others through service? What is my purpose?
- And finally ask yourself: What am I grateful for? What do I feel grateful for as I center into my heart? What am I grateful for?
- Now, take a deep breath and let go of those questions. And quietly sit in silence.

And when you are ready, bring your awareness back to this space. Thanks for doing our first meditation together!

PART ONE

# Understanding the Roots of Personal Philosophies and Values

# CHAPTER 1

# Embracing People of All Backgrounds

*"Cultural differences should not separate us from each other,
but rather cultural diversity brings a collective strength that can
benefit all of humanity."*
— *Robert Alan*

*"Someone asked me what is your religion?" I said,
"All the paths that lead to the light."*
— *Sneha Maheswari*

WHEN I AM ASKED WHAT my tradition is, I often say: "I am an Inclusiastic. I include everyone." Being Inclusiastic, to me, means being compassionate and all-embracing. It means celebrating all traditions and welcoming people who hail from all backgrounds.

There is a great perk to being Inclusiastic: You get to hang out with people of all cultures and faiths, and learn from them. One of the most powerful lessons is this: Most traditions share undeniable similarities and people are not as "different" as we may assume they are. I believe we are all world citizens connected by our humanity.

I am a firm believer that we can benefit by reaching outside the circle of family and learn from people from other backgrounds. We might even choose to explore or blend in the tenets or beliefs of philosophies that appeal to us. For example, while I was raised in a Christian household, I've also been drawn to Buddhism, Taoism, and Eastern philosophies. And while I studied psychology and interfaith ministry, I also have a passion for science. I often say that if I were a tree, my trunk would be Christian and Buddhist and my branches would be Jewish, Hindu, Sufi, and many other world traditions.

I have never believed that one thing must preclude the other. We can embrace many influences and studies at once over the course of our lifetimes. Some of us struggle or feel stuck in a certain way of being, or we may feel limited by some of the messages of our upbringing, but if we are open to learning new things it can lead to evolution and change.

## Different Cultural Ideas Can Shape Us

My dad was an engineer so we moved around—a lot—when I was young. In fact, traveling was a family tradition. I was born in Idaho, but lived in Oregon, Washington, California, Michigan, Florida, Belgium and Italy, and I moved to New York at age twenty. While it was sad to lose friends and have to start over, I learned to easily adapt to change. It was also a great blessing to be exposed to so many different parts of the country at such an early age. It opened my eyes to the fact that there were so many people in the world that were not like my nuclear family. The world was filled with people who had different beliefs, came from different cultures, and hailed from many ethnic backgrounds. They ate different foods, danced certain dances, and sometimes spoke with accents or in a different language. I learned early to embrace and celebrate people from different traditions, and I feel very fortunate for these experiences because they help define who I am today.

My penchant for "Inclusiasm" set me up to become a world traveler. It was another blessing in my life that I was able to see so much of this amazing world and connect with so many people as I traveled for work and leisure. I cherish the opportunity to study the nuances of so many cultures and see how people live in their day-to-day lives around the world.

## The Monks Who Walked into My Life

My life truly changed when I was introduced to a group of Tibetan Buddhist Monks, led by Geshe Lobsang Tenzin Negi, PhD, from the Drepung Loseling *Monastery*, who became my dear friend over two decades years ago, and who led me to the teachings of His Holiness the Dalai Lama. Meeting the monks and Dr. Negi—whom I affectionately address as "Geshe-La"—changed my life. They now call me "Acha-La," which means revered sister. They were the first teachers to show me how to meditate and go within, and they helped me step onto a spiritual path that led to the journey of exploration and spiritual growth that brought me to this moment.

I have been devoted to my meditation practice for many years, and it has helped me stay balanced even in the most difficult times. It has also proven to me that with practice, we can grow, change, and improve our lives. Along the way, I have been drawn to many spiritual studies, but I have engaged most deeply with the philosophies of Taoism and Buddhism. The main reason is that both are extremely open-minded and incline heavily towards philosophy rather than being based on dogma.

I have also participated in much professional training to improve my ability to help others; this includes being ordained as an interfaith minister in 1998, graduating from a counseling program at the University of Santa Monica, taking grief and loss trainings and attending a two-year inter-spiritual wisdom course through Spiritual Paths Wisdom Institute.

I know that in real life we must take time out for family and work. I understand how distracted we can become by everyday life and how overwhelmed we can get while caregiving for others. But I truly believe that when the student is ready the teacher appears. And that when we are open we will be given life lessons that help us grow. When we allow ourselves to learn more about how others live and identify our own true passions, we can activate new aspects of our being. This expands our personal philosophy.

## Follow Your Own Passion

Once I opened my mind and heart, my hunger for more spiritual wisdom never subsided. I loved learning spirituality from other cultures, but I did not need to convert to any other tradition that called to me. What I found on my path were tools to be happier, which happened to hail from different parts of the world than the area I was raised in.

By the same token, my spiritual explorations did not interfere with my other emerging interests. For example, I developed a keen interest in philosophy, science, and how the brain works. I did not feel called to go to school to become a neuroscientist, but I am fascinated about the ways in which the human brain developed and how our minds operate. I have loved learning and blending the soulful and the intellectual aspects of life, the spiritual and the scientific, and I love exploring where the paths intersect. This has enhanced and expanded my personal philosophy.

Every road I have taken has led me to understand some of the most important keys to life, including what I see as the most crucial in our world today: That we must love and have compassion for one another. And ourselves. This is a theme I will revisit often in this book.

## Embracing Everyone

When I was a child in school, I was taught that America was a great nation, a "melting pot," because it was comprised of peoples of all nationalities from all over the world. Our country has always welcomed others. Lady Liberty, a beacon for all newcomers, stands on a pedestal emblazoned with a plaque beginning with the words, "Give me your tired, your poor, your huddled masses, yearning to breathe free."

Obviously, my personal philosophy was greatly expanded by my deep study of Asian philosophies, which are founded on the basic premise that we are all connected and interdependent. They have helped me see that even though no one overtly sets out to be selfish, we still live within the confines of ourselves, our families and our social circles. Many of us are largely cut off from the needs or suffering of those outside our environment. We are separated by neighborhoods and social status. But even if we cannot see someone else's suffering firsthand, we can still wish for them to be free of suffering, just as we wish that for ourselves.

Here's what I truly believe: When we develop a deep, profound love, an unconditional love for all human beings, this creates a space in one's heart for people who hold different beliefs. When we are true to ourselves and have a place in our hearts for others, it transcends tolerance and acceptance. It's a calling and a way of being—a life philosophy.

It's up to people who have had the opportunity to season and exercise this part of themselves to make it more widely available. Those who have made progress on this must help others figure out how to see the importance of a powerful, inclusive love for all human beings in the world today. As a global society we need to look at this issue. I believe that our hearts and minds want to experience the peace of embracing all people rather than the pain of carrying hatred and separation.

I'm not saying it's easy. In today's busy world, we get distracted and we may not always have the support we need from those around us. But we have to summon courage. We must push away the fear that, just because someone hails from a different culture or looks different, we should exclude them. I believe there is a way to break through with profound love and compassion. It's what I call loving kindness and equanimity.

In my heart of hearts, I believe we are an evolving species and we can all make ourselves better human beings with a little practice and awareness. That's where science and spirituality work in tandem. There's a need to keep learning, exploring, asking questions, and evolving. As we do more inner work, we can improve our ability to discern the real truth from inaccurate news of the day. With time we can create an intuitive approach that will determine our personal truth.

## A Reverence for Life

There are many influences that shape our personal philosophies as we grow up. If we are exposed to experiences beyond "our own little worlds," they may broaden our view and teach us a new way of seeing things.

My parents were so clearly the foundation of my own personal philosophy on life. They gave me the tools to navigate the world and to expand on all they taught me. I came to the idea about being "Inclusiastic" through something I learned from my father and mother. It is called "a reverence for life." This is a concept my parents adopted from the Christian minister, philosopher, and medical doctor Albert Schweitzer, who famously said: "Ethics is nothing other than reverence for life. Reverence for life affords me my fundamental principle of morality, namely, that good consists in maintaining, assisting and enhancing life, and to destroy, to harm or to hinder life is evil." Helping others was imperative to Schweitzer.

This is not something attained through the study of any philosophy or social science. It is the basic innate understanding of essential virtues and ideas, and how they are expressed uniquely, by every individual, in how we live our lives. This was not taught to me in words but from the example my father and mother showed me by how they lived their lives.

While I acknowledge and rejoice in the things we humans share and have in common, I am also excited and fascinated by our differences. We are the same in many ways, especially in our intrinsic value and the fact that we all deserve to pursue happiness in the way we feel we can best arrive at that goal. But every human being is still undeniably unique, and that is absolutely fascinating to me.

Learning about different cultures and meeting so many people with stories to share has been a driving force in my life. As a result I have learned so many philosophies that originated in different parts of the world. With open hearts and open minds, we can all be "Inclusiastics," trusting that Divine Love and Spirit will give us strength and support to open our hearts and minds to diversity and inclusivity.

# CHAPTER 2

# How Our Personal Philosophies Develop

*"The outer world is a reflection of the inner world. Other people's perception of you is a reflection of them; your response to them is an awareness of you."*
— *Roy T. Bennett*

PEOPLE TEND TO THINK OF philosophy as a topic they are forced to study in school or something they read in a history or mythology book. *The Oxford English Dictionary describes it as* "the study of the fundamental nature of knowledge, reality, and existence, especially when considered as an academic discipline" and "the study of the theoretical basis of a particular branch of knowledge or experience." But the concept of philosophy is not just about ancient musings from Aristotle and Socrates.

My life centers on philosophy, and we all have our own personal philosophies on life; and some of our conclusions about the nature of reality are just as profound as the most famous masters of philosophical thought who have pondered human existence over the eons. In fact, many people build businesses, careers, and movements based on their personal philosophies. They write, speak about, and promote them on social media, and they encourage others to agree with their point of view.

There are many other people who have strong and heartfelt personal philosophies that they choose to hold close to the vest.

They may not share their ideas publicly or even proclaim them to be a life philosophy, yet they may build their lives around these beliefs and simply live as closely as possible to the core of what is most important to them. They are conscious of who they are, and what they are about, but don't feel the need to shout it out. People around them often understand who these people are based on their manner and behavior.

Then there is a segment of people in our world who do not possess an awareness of their own personal philosophy. They live by it, via automatic response and habit, but it typically manifests in their behavior without a clear understanding of their own emotional and mental makeup. These beliefs become prescriptions for living, but are not in the person's conscious awareness. The challenge with this is that people are driven to certain behaviors and experiences, but they have no idea why. They are also more malleable and vulnerable to the influence of others who have stronger ideas or who are bullies. This can lead people to get involved with individuals, experiences, and movements that don't have their best interest at heart and can also lead to feeling aimless and unclear about what they should be doing in life.

Or it can lead to bad decision-making.

Humans spend their lives making choices, reacting, and sometimes being swayed to do things based on the needs of (or pressure from) others. The bottom line is we are constantly taking actions, small and large, based on a decision or some kind of motivation. These decisions do not come out of thin air, with no reasons behind them. They come from a set of basic ideas, opinions, beliefs and attitudes that are ingrained within us— whether we know it or not!

## Shining a Light on Underlying Factors

There are many things in a person's life that influence their personal philosophy. Many of them occur very early in life, and some evolve as a person grows. Having an inkling of what these are can help people understand the things that may sway the way they look at life or the beliefs they hold. These are just some of the significant influences that go into shaping our underlying point-of-view on life.

## Influences Growing Up

**PARENTS AND CAREGIVERS.** The first influences on our personal philosophies have to do with the way our parents raised us and what they imparted to us as children. They teach us things that begin to formulate our earliest opinions. Most importantly, they shape us through words, actions, and what they model to us.

**SIBLINGS AND FAMILY.** The way a family unit lives and functions puts down the ground work for our worldview. Relationships with siblings impact us greatly, whether they are great relationships or not so great. We may also have cousins, aunts, and grandparents who cast a strong influence. We formulate other relationships in the world based on what occurred in our household. Until we have an awareness of this, it is often an unconscious drive to recreate the family we grew up with—for better or for worse.

**ENVIRONMENT.** There continues to be a debate about nature versus nurture—whether our genetics and hereditary aspects or environmental variables play a bigger role in human development. However, studies clearly show that the environment in which we are raised has a huge impact on who we become. Where we lived, our surrounding culture, things we experienced and were exposed to, and social relationships truly help shape us. If the environment has some level of instability and lacks safety, it shapes us in different ways.

**CULTURE AND ETHNICITY.** The cultural and ethnic aspects of our upbringing are woven into the fabric of our lives. From the foods we eat, to the dances we dance, to expressions and words that we heard growing up, culture bonds us in a common experience with others. It gives us a point of view about life, death, celebrations, family, relationships, and what is meaningful in life. It provides a common ground and consciousness with a community. It also offers a common understanding of injustice, prejudice, danger, violence, micro-aggression, the experience of being "other," and intergenerational trauma. Various cultures and ethnicities may share a common history of abuse and a deep memory of pain that shape personal philosophy.

**FRIENDS AND SOCIAL RELATIONSHIPS.** Childhood, tweenage, and teenage friends have a deep influence on the formation of our early philosophies on life, but these change as we grow. We move through stages of life in which family is not the center of influence and friends, peers and social alliances become paramount, and peer pressure may dominate. It's in those times that we may bend to the pressure of others or find our own voices.

**ROMANTIC PARTNERS.** We go through natural stages in life where we long for love, attention, and union with another. We search and we sometimes settle down. People will cross our romantic paths and we will quickly forget them. Others will leave an indelible mark—some in a good way and others in a negative way, if there was abuse, unkindness, or abandonment. But each significant relationship will add to our philosophy on love and life. The most significant of these will impact us for a lifetime: first loves, biggest loves, forever loves, and the ones who left us or did not treat us well.

**EDUCATION.** Early education has a big influence on how we learn and how we see ourselves. Good teachers help us through the rough spots. Schoolmates and peers exert much pressure in those early years. Many people just try to hang on and survive. If you have to move around a lot, as I did, it's hard to make friends and maintain school relationships. By the time we get to college, there's a new set of influences, social and academic. But college and graduate school are also a time of developing new skills, reaching a completely new understanding of the way the world works, and expanding our brains. Maybe there is a very special teacher who helps you become who you are meant to be. And yes, we may possibly take a philosophy class.

**WORK AND CAREER.** Some people see work as a means to an end, a tolerable job that pays the bills. Others seek out work that has personal meaning. Some take time out from work outside the home to raise families. Others are focused primarily on building their careers and establishing themselves in their chosen field. No matter how someone pursues their work life path, it impacts their personal philosophy. As in romance and friendship, the most significant work experiences—good and bad—will stay with us.

**HEALTH AND FAMILY HEATH.** People who are relatively healthy and fit have a different view and experience in life from those who suffered through childhood illnesses or were traumatized by the illness of a sibling, parent, or grandparent. Chronic illness or disability shapes life in a way that people who have never had to face that cannot truly comprehend. Ill health or disability of a parent, or terminal illness, also has a strong impact on personal philosophy.

**MEDIA, ADVERTISING, AND BOOKS.** The media pervades everything we do and influences us in powerful and subtle ways. New stories and current events can transform us ("First human walks on the moon!") and traumatize us ("World Trade Center towers fall!"). By the same token, many books leave a lasting impression. They inspire new beliefs and can become part of the fabric of our lives. Studies show that fictional characters can influence our real lives, as role models or maybe even by moving us to name a child after a favorite character. Just as some commercials and magazine ads can inspire us to want to improve our lives, advertising can also influence us in negative ways. Studies have shown that girls start losing self-esteem at an early age due to exposure to models and movie stars whose air-blown perfection makes them feel inadequate.

**ERA.** The time in history in which we were born has a great impact on how we experience and perceive life. They say that history is cyclical, but it never quite happens as it did before and we are all shaped by the things that impacted "our generation." Many of us had parents who grew up in the Depression and had a certain way of preserving everything due to the lack they knew in childhood. Baby Boomers, Generation X, Y (Millennials), and Z all face different realities and share certain beliefs and experiences. Being aware of where others are coming from is a key to getting along, but many people face a generation gap within their own families. Intergenerational interactions can impact a person's philosophy.

**TRAVEL.** Seeing the world, traveling for business, and taking vacations can leave a huge imprint. Having a chance to explore other cultures and learn how other people live and love is a powerful experience. It can make you feel like a part of the world, can relax you, and can be educational on so many levels. By the same token, being forced to fly too much for business, having a bad experience with a certain cultural destination, or being fearful of travel can also shape your view.

## Psychological Aspects

**PERSONALITY.** There are several schools of thought on the development of the human personality. It is essentially a combination of temperament and a collection of habits, responses, and ways of thinking that a person uses to navigate through life. For example, a child may be introverted and shy or be the extroverted life of the party at the playground. One school of personality theory holds that each individual has a unique psychological structure that makes them one of a kind, while others believe individuals have comparable and similar traits. Experts say you can begin to see the personality developing early on in life and yet the personality may continue to develop into adolescence. Most importantly, anything can happen along the way to shape the personality, including traumas.

**ATTACHMENT PATTERNS.** Attachment patterns evolved from the way we are treated by parents or significant others in the earliest months after birth. If a parent is loving and attentive and we bond well, we feel taken care of. If a parent is emotionally distant or absent, we feel unsafe and abandoned. These early experiences become imbedded into us before we reach a year old, and the attachment patterns will impact the way we see ourselves for life, unless we develop an awareness of them.

**EARLY TRAUMA.** Exposure to any category or level of neglect and abuse can impact an individual in a myriad of ways. It is very common for someone who has been hurt as a child to develop mental health issues. They may suffer from depression and generalized anxiety. They may self-harm or turn to addictive substances. They may develop a viewpoint of being unworthy or see themselves as victims.

**EXPOSURE TRAUMA.** In the course of the day there are many ways that average people are exposed to disturbing events, often simply by listening to the news or seeing the replay of graphic images on the internet. Hearing about awful things secondhand can make you sad, angry, or afraid and can lead you to try to quell or avoid the feelings with addictive substances or avoidance strategies.

**UNRESOLVED TRAUMA.** People can get stuck in the past and the pain of their early years. This trauma may have happened once, but it can be triggered over and over. This can impact a person's personal philosophy, in that they may build a wall around them to protect themselves. This also leads people to try to self-soothe with alcohol and drugs, which hinder a person's ability to know themselves.

**UNCONSCIOUS MIND.** Sigmund Freud's psychoanalytic theory revealed the idea that the mind has a sublevel basement that stores old memories, traumas, hurts, urges, and feelings. It is like a reservoir of material that exists somewhere beyond our conscious awareness. These are typically unpleasant memories or feelings or things that we consider unacceptable, shameful, painful, or related to conflict. Shining a light on these things by exploring, acknowledging, and naming them can help us move on. But when these remain hidden, they lead to behaviors and reactions that may be unhealthy.

## Spiritual and Soul Influences

**RELIGION AND FAITH.** People who possess a deep faith tend to feel empowered by it in many areas of life. Studies show people with strong religious beliefs who pray may heal faster. A recent Pew Research Center study showed that people who are highly religious are more engaged with their extended families, more likely to volunteer, more involved in their communities, and generally happier with the way things are going in their lives.

**LACK OF FAITH.** People who grew up feeling oppressed by the religion they were born into, or were forced by parents to go to worship services, often emerge with a different kind of reality when it comes to faith. They may observe religion out of guilt or pressure, or they may abandon it completely, along with their belief in God. Atheists do not see a contradiction between atheism and pondering their place in the world. Pew Research reports that about a third of American atheists say they think about the meaning and purpose of life at least weekly. Atheists, agnostics, and undecided individuals tend to formulate a personal philosophy based on the experience of what is personally meaningful outside of the realm of tradition.

**ADOPTED FAITH.** Many people acquire a life philosophy based on a tradition they came across, were exposed to, and fell in love with. For example, many of today's Buddhists were not born into this tradition. They developed interest because they found food for the soul and spiritual comfort. Or, they practice both their religion of birth and adopted traditions. As Rabbi Joseph Gelberman, founder of The New Seminary, used to say, "Never instead of, always in addition to." Some people embrace interfaith and multifaith spirituality because they love the richness of being able to choose what they love about each tradition.

**SPIRITUAL PATH.** Some people find themselves walking a spiritual path unlike anyone they know. They may meditate or do yoga. They may be called to a monastery, seminary, or ashram. They may get a hug from the guru Ammachi or find themselves in the presence of His Holiness the Dalai Lama. They may see a vast array of ways to worship, experience life, or serve. They may speak to the Divine as God, Goddess, Great Spirit of All There Is, or simply consider there is a power that connects us all together that they refer to as The

Universe, Spirit, or the Holy Spirit. They may not even call their spiritual path anything in particular, yet they walk it each day.

## Are There Problematic Philosophies?

Philosophies are problematic if they endanger life, negate human rights, and cause harm. I feel strongly there are certain behaviors that are unacceptable. We live in a world where there is too much violence and cult-like behavior, and I do not condone the personal philosophy of someone who hurts others intentionally. In my personal philosophy, non-violence and other values are sacred.

But I have to balance that with my belief that all humans must be free to make their own decisions. One of the reasons that I love America is that our Constitution espouses the idea that people should be free in countless ways; that we have freedom of speech and freedom of religion. We are supposed to respect others' rights to worship as they choose or follow any political party. We are free to think for ourselves and, even, free to have our own personal philosophies.

I encourage people to make a conscious decision to explore their personal philosophy and to determine if it is something they are choosing to live by or if it is simply driving them.

Ultimately, none of us can tell another person what to believe. They must think for themselves. Of course, they can hear the opinions of others, but in the end, they must decide for themselves how to live their lives and how to treat others.

Ask yourself: Do you have an underlying understanding of what makes you tick, or is your philosophy composed of a patchwork quilt of beliefs based on what others told you to believe or what you hear on television?

When people follow blindly without questioning they can get lost in a belief system that is not truly aligned with their truth. They may even find their values and principles eroded by following philosophies and leaders that do not have the best interest of our world in mind. One of my close friends was world renowned pediatrician, Dr. Lee Salk, and he used to say, "The demise of values is the demise of society." When we do not take the time to discern our true values, we may end up living someone else's.

Give some thought to your personal philosophy. You will have a chance to dive more deeply into this topic at the end of the book in the final exercise, "Creating a Life Philosophy that Brings You Joy."

## CHAPTER 3

# Where Do Core Values and Principles Come From?

*"The person, who knows the principles of life and observes them, has a strong foundation in life."*
— *Sunday Adelaja*

I BELIEVE THAT HUMANS, BY THEIR very nature, need a personal philosophy. Everyone needs a way to blend in aspects of our common humanity with personal, treasured beliefs. This becomes a blueprint for living.

To live a life of self-awareness we also have to take a deep look at our underlying values and principles. They are a driving force in formulating our personal philosophies, and they also connect (or disconnect) us to humanity. We may be unique and individual, but we share core values with other humans. For example, most people want to:

- Have basic needs fulfilled
- Experience happiness
- Be loved
- Have a community
- Be able to make sense of the world
- Make a difference in the world (or their world of family and community)

- Live a life that has meaning and purpose

Of course, we all have a different view on what is meaningful and what it means to be happy. People often compare themselves to others and imagine that making a difference in the world requires coming up with a cure for cancer or a polio vaccine. I am reminded again of my friend Dr. Lee Salk, who healed so many children and helped so many parents. He was also the brother of Jonas Salk, who developed the polio vaccine. They both made an extraordinary difference in the world. But I also know mothers who've nurtured sick children back to health, people who care for elderly parents, and teachers who are helping to shape the future in local schools. You don't have to come up with a cure for a pandemic or be a world leader to make a difference.

If you want your life to have meaning, you have to tap into the part of you that believes you have a purpose for being on earth and to commit yourself to identifying it—or creating it. But first, consider the inner influences that give you personal power or keep you stuck in old patterns, lead you to deny your own truth to please others, or have caused you to forsake values of importance.

## Looking at Values

When was the last time you paused to think about the principles and values you hold dear? In our hectic world I would bet it has been a while. I'd like to encourage you to take a moment to think about them now.

Let me kick it off by sharing the original source of my own core values. I believe it will help others to think about the early life experiences that shaped what ultimately became the building blocks of their philosophy on life.

I grew up in a family that thrived on being principled. My father, whom I adored, was very clear about what was right and what was wrong. There were no gray areas. My sister, brother and I did not lie, steal, or cheat because it was part of our family dynamic to be honest, generous, and stay clear of unethical behaviors.

Because honesty was one of our cherished family traits, as a kid, I was taught to tell the truth even if I did something wrong or embarrassing. We weren't berated when we fessed up to our shortcomings; we were encouraged to reflect on all aspects of the situation, to assess our own behavior, and to come up with a solution.

I also grew up knowing that family was the most important part of life because my father set a very strong example of the importance of loyalty to your loved ones. My dad constantly impressed upon us that our family relationships strengthened us. And that my siblings and I were best friends who would always be loyal, trustworthy, and supportive. We were taught to offer this to extended family, good friends, and trusted business associates.

Dad was my guiding light. He was my original wisdom teacher. He made sure the parameters of right and wrong were very clearly defined for us. He taught me how to take the pulse of principles in every situation and to do the right thing, even when it was unpopular or brought on criticism.

I was so young when he died, only nineteen, and I wish I had more time with him to guide me along the path of life. I was lucky that my mother stepped in as family matriarch and carried on Dad's beliefs and principles in our family life until we lost her at eighty-four years old.

I believe my father gave me the tools I needed to formulate my principled approach to life's opportunities and challenges. And my mother enforced them and supported me along the way. But the time came for me to carve my own path. While my path—as all our paths are—was built with the bricks from early childhood and the ethics and wisdom of parents, we continue to add on to our original beliefs.

I continued the path my parents set forth for me by finding things that nurtured my heart, mind, and spirit; things that not just supported my core values but made them stronger. It led me to meditation, self-awareness, and spiritual practices that have been ongoing for many years. It led me to learn as much as I could about how to strengthen core values—rather than have them depleted by life—and to try to build my life around them. Nothing is perfect. While principles remain the same, life is always a work in progress. I was blessed to have many role models along the way who inspired me.

## Life Lessons That Shape Us

There are many things that shape us as we grow. One of the most important lessons of my lifetime is this: As adults, we find ourselves viewing life through a particular lens and living through a specific personal philosophy. Some people continue on the path of principles and others are influenced by other factors along the way. Some people have experienced less than supportive early childhoods, and have never been taught the basic principles of life that were standard in generations before. Then there are those people that choose an unprincipled life based on deceit, greed, and benefiting at the expense of others; they make no distinction between what is ethical and what is not.

Another time in my life I would have believed there was little hope for people with no moral compass. Now I embrace the idea that when we focus on self-awareness we can grow all that is good inside us and transform behaviors that erode decency in our world.

I find that in today's society, very few people are stopping to critically think about what their values, principles, and beliefs are. But consider this: Since they drive your life, aren't they worth defining a little bit? If you don't pause to evaluate or think about it, you may be like a sailboat without a rudder. You're out there floating around on the ocean with nothing to help you steer.

People sometimes mistake values, principles, and a moral compass with spirituality. Those aspects of your life may indeed be influenced by spiritual beliefs or faith, but they also exist in everyone. Whether Christian or Buddhist, atheist, or agnostic, we are all living with some kind of belief system that is a driving force. It formulates our personal ethics—or lack thereof—and often moves us to go to bat for, argue about, or insist on certain things that we believe in strongly. Too often, we are not even aware why we do what we do. It's a pattern. A habit. A way of being.

If you get to *know yourself* on a deeper level, you may discover there is also a collective consciousness at work at all times.

## Question Everything

Take a moment to ponder these important questions and to ask yourself, "What are the greatest influences of my childhood?"

- How have my parents guided or influenced my principles?
- How were my grandparents a source of wisdom or insight?
- How did religion, culture, ethnicity, or location of birth shape me?
- Was there a personal or family trauma or loss that impacted my views on life?
- Did childhood dreams inspire certain beliefs?
- Who are my role models today, personal and professional?
- What are some of the ethics I believe in?
- What are my core values as an adult?
- What are my most important principles?
- Where is my moral compass?
- What core beliefs rule my life?
- What is my personal philosophy on life?
- What did I believe as a child that I wish I could still believe today?
- What do I wish there was more of in the world?
- What is most important to me?

Basic psychology tells us we are all driven by unconscious aspects of ourselves. Some beliefs are so old and hidden, we may not be aware that they are operating in our lives. There are scripts and messages formed in childhood that are so much a part of us that they are automatic.

Answering the questions is designed to help you mine personal insights. What would happen if you dug a little deeper to understand the full, true driving force that is your life's philosophy? You may come to know yourself on the deepest level and learn how to continue to grow with each new experience in life. You might find the wherewithal to unpack some of your life's mysteries and challenges and begin to heal them at the root. You might even be able to access all the beliefs that have brought you to this moment and then learn to nurture them and enhance them.

Most importantly, you may find the strength to operate in life from your most cherished principles and find truer happiness and strength in doing so.

## Preserving Our Principles

In a world filled with temptations and demands to negate your own values, how do you stand strong and not make concessions? When there are so many people around who lack character and operate without scruples, how do you hold fast to your own moral center? When pressures from people, work life, and society try to bend your value to fit their needs, how do you stay on a path of purpose where you are true to your own heart?

I am not going to say it is always easy for us humans to rise to every occasion and fight for what we believe at all times. But we can engage in a process of personal growth and positive practices that can help us stay centered and that allow us to focus our energy on those things we truly hold dear.

The first step is self-awareness and a willingness to understand the life experiences that formed you and those that may have influenced you along the way. The second step is to open your mind to learning new practices that expand your awareness and understanding. And the third step is to make choices about how you want to live your life today.

If you compromise a principle, it no longer exists. But that doesn't mean you can't transform your life and establish new or revised principles. My hope is that you allow yourself compassion as you embark on the journey of discovery and growth.

# CHAPTER 4

# Why Compassion Is So Important

*"Be kind, for everyone you meet may be fighting a battle you
know nothing about."*
*— Rev. Dr. John Watson*

I HAVE ALWAYS CONSIDERED MYSELF A good person
who was kind and helpful. But I did not truly have the tools
to offer healing to myself and others until I learned to harness
the power of compassion.

Embracing compassion opened my awareness to a whole new
level of understanding. It is now the foundation of my life and it
has led me to trust that it is the salve needed to heal ourselves and
the world. But I know that it can take people some time to warm
up to the concept of compassion. I had so many questions about it
myself in the beginning that it led me on a search to find out more.
I wondered: *What is compassion? Are we born compassionate?
Can we cultivate it? If so, how?*

People struggle with the concept of compassion and sometimes
feel that it should not be distributed equally. For example, we
may have compassion for a sick child, but why should we be
compassionate toward someone who seems better off than we are
and seems to have no problems? Or someone who is greedy, or
who has hurt or injured us?

At first glance, it may seem that compassion is only something that certain people can offer and only certain people deserve, but I believe compassion is the great equalizer. It is something anyone can experience and offer. It is uplifting and freeing. It saves us from being emotionally imprisoned by our own negative thoughts about other people and ourselves. It urges us to consider the plights and the hardship of others before rushing to judgment.

My mom used to say, "You cannot judge other people because you have not walked in their shoes." We truly have no idea what other people have gone through or how it has affected them. We can never assume to know the joys or the pain they may be carrying. We can never fully grasp the reasons behind their behavior and actions, certainly not by witnessing only one moment in time as opposed to the big picture. Circumstances sometimes afford us only a limited view of why someone may do or say something.

Unless you walk in someone else's shoes, you do not have enough information to judge.

You may see a well-dressed man who seems to have it all, based on his clothes, attractiveness, and his polished and professional look. You may think to yourself, he has it made. But you may not see his pain. Perhaps he was abused as a child, just went through a miserable divorce, or has lost a child or a parent to cancer and feels broken inside.

Teenagers may judge each other, perhaps picking on the new kid in school. Little do they know this beautiful young lady lost her brother and grandmother in a violent crime or that her parents neglected her completely? She had to raise herself and live with a distant aunt who was never home. Also, the "mean girls" may be jealous, and acting out in a terrible way to mask their own deep pain.

I have witnessed adults hoarding supplies in an emergency situation or acting unkindly to people less fortunate, often out of fear. Some people judge others as "less successful" or they judge people who are "more successful." What is "success" anyway? Success to me is being kind, compassionate, and carving out a meaningful journey here on this planet.

## You Can Practice Compassion

Just as practicing piano will make you a better musician, practicing compassion can make you a better human. As with a musical instrument or driving, kindness and compassion can be learned. What you practice, you become. Neuroscientists say you can develop new brain pathways by practicing kindness and compassion. If you practice kindness and happiness, you will be a kinder and happier person. It can help you let go of your negative habits and create new, positive habits that will turn your life into a happier one.

We are all so busy and sometimes we feel that our lives are not as fulfilling or rewarding as we would like them to be. We all deserve happiness, but we often struggle with how to create more of it in our lives. The path of compassion offers lasting joy and meaning.

## Cultivating Compassion

So how do we cultivate our compassionate hearts? By recognizing everyone on this planet has a story. No one has it "all," and everyone has endured some type of pain or hardship whether they are a successful businessman or an hourly wage immigrant who is striving to support a family. Compassion and kindness are the opposite of envy, jealousy, hatred, and lack of empathy. It allows us to look into the eyes of another and truly see them.

The dictionary tells us:
*Compassion is "sympathy and concern for the sufferings or misfortunes of others."*

*Kindness is "the quality of being friendly, generous, and considerate."*

I would add a loving heart to the definition of compassion and kindness. I believe we have to visualize and feel our hearts becoming softer, allowing us to open to the loving, gentler side that we all have. We can exercise this part of us with right- thinking and meditation.

In psychology there is a term called active listening, which means you really listen to the other's point of view to establish true congruency and empathy with and for the other person. This is related to compassion because compassion also requires us to truly listen to the other's point of view in order to create a better perspective and point of view.

What if we could walk in the shoes of a refugee who is fleeing their country with their family to avoid persecution? What if we walked in the shoes of a teenager who has been sexually abused and tried to understand the pain and violation? What if we were respectful to the fact that every human being is on a journey, and what if we honored that journey by not judging them?

We simply do not have enough information to judge.

## Compassion at Home

One night I yelled at my twenty-year-old daughter because she stayed up until 2 a.m. chatting with a friend. She had to wake up at 7 a.m. for an appointment, and I was upset that she was not going to get enough sleep. I allowed myself to get angry, rationalizing it was because I love her and care about her health. I thought staying up late would ruin her morning. Her response was, "Mom, don't go to bed angry."

My night owl child's admonishment to not end the day in a negative state of mind reminded me of what my parents used to tell me: *Never go to sleep angry and never have unresolved, incomplete issues with those you love. What if you never see them again? Don't separate from those you love without telling them how you feel and how much you love them.* So I told my daughter I was worried she would be rundown and become ill. She explained that her friend was going through a family issue and needed her advice. We sorted it all out so that no one had to stuff anger under the covers.

Completion leads us to compassion. As my dad said to my siblings and me, over and over, "It's more important to be loving and compassionate than to be right." I was right about my daughter needing sleep, but being angry didn't help either one of us. Actively listening to my daughter helped me walk in her shoes and understand that she was being a good friend. She was practicing compassion.

We are *all* wisdom teachers. We can learn from each other. When my daughter told me not to go to bed angry, she was my wisdom teacher. We all have wisdom to share with one another. We can learn from each other if we are open to this experience. We can learn from everyone we meet, especially when we remove judgment.

## Doing the Best They Can

The old adage, "There are two sides to every story" is very true. I believe to some degree that most people you come across in daily life are doing the best they can with the resources they have available. This includes physical, mental, emotional, financial as well as environmental, nutritional, and health resources—or lack thereof.

If they really knew a better way, they would be doing that. We are all constantly learning and, indeed, can learn something new every day—including how to become more compassionate.

I believe it is our responsibility as humans to try to have compassion for everyone we meet. Even with an extensive view of someone's background, motives, and feelings, one can never be sure what someone else is going through because sometimes they themselves do not understand. Therefore, we cannot assume or deny someone's motives or behavior. We should not pass judgment on another person or how they handle certain situations.

Not long ago I saw a woman dressed in traditional burka and noticed many people averting their eyes, as if they were afraid to look in her direction. I truly don't believe that what makes us visually and culturally different in appearance has any bearing on who we are inside. We are each given a heart, brain, body, breath, and spirit. We each have hopes, dreams, fears, and desires to be happy. I know that I don't have a true understanding of the life she may lead, but I felt called to let her know that it didn't matter. I just smiled and offered a quiet hello, because smiling changes everything. It allows you to access your heart, where we truly are the same.

There is an exhibit at the National Liberty Museum in Philadelphia that drives home this point to children—and adults. It is a huge, clear box filled with millions of jelly beans. In front of this clear box stands a statue that looks like a person made of jelly beans. Next to the statue is a sign that asks people to ponder how humans and jelly beans are similar. The answer is that we come in all different colors, shapes, and sizes on the outside but inside is the same. The jelly bean can come in a wide assortment of colors and shades, but the inner part is always made the same way.

Many times we look at the outside of something or the outcome of a situation and jump to a conclusion about why or how it is the way it is. Even people who do harmful things may have a story of trauma that explains their behavior. We may not care about their pain and we may think them evil, but it is possible to condemn someone's actions and still feel compassion for their soul. Many people remember Pope John II visiting the man who shot him four times and nearly killed him, to show him mercy and forgiveness. Compassion allows average people to show mercy to one another.

## We Are Interconnected

Humans have always possessed a survival mechanism that has enabled us to harness nature, create societies, push into new territories, and conquer land. Over time this has created a society where adversarial and competitive tendencies are more pronounced, and it has created distance where there was once commonality. But we always have, and always will, rely on one another in ways we often don't stop to think about, until a crisis hits or an event occurs that requires us to work together for the common good. We may live in different towns or countries, but we are all connected through our humanity. Our hearts beat. We breathe. We grieve. We give birth. We die and lose others. We live in political and economic systems. All societies are tied together. We *are* one world.

Astronaut Gene Cernan walked on the moon during his Apollo 17 mission and he had the chance to see our universe from a unique perspective. He once explained it to me this way: "From space, you look down and see our world, an island of blue in a sea of black space," he said. "Imagine all the people living on this round globe. We all wish to be free from suffering, to be happy. We are here for such a short time. Maybe one-hundred years if we are very lucky. We are here together. Can't we be kind, loving, and compassionate toward each other since we all share the common goal of existing without suffering?"

Understanding how interconnected we are allows us to feel more compassion for those around us—those we know and those we may never meet. It may start with curiosity and a desire for basic understanding on an intellectual level. Then it may move into the emotional realm. Soon it can reach the heart. You may be surprised how your entire being can fill up with compassion.

But on this journey of opening our hearts to others, it is imperative that we also learn to feel compassion for ourselves. Chances are, if we are judging other people, we are judging ourselves—a lot. The more accepting we are of others, the more accepting we can be of ourselves, and vice-versa. We are connected in more ways than we realize, and understanding this is the beginning of accessing a deeper sense of compassion.

## The Pencil

Take the example of a simple pencil. There isn't a single person in the world who could make a pencil all by themselves. Sound crazy? Not really. Consider that the wood for a common number two pencil is cedar, which came from the Great Lakes in America. In order to cut the wood, you need a saw. To make a saw you need steel. To make steel you need iron ore from Brazil. The part in the center, the part we call lead, is actually graphite. It was imported from Sri Lanka, mixed with clay and wax. The clay is from Southern United States and the wax is from Mexico.

The metal piece, which holds the eraser to the wood, is made of zinc and copper. The zinc is from Canada and the copper came from Chile. The eraser is made from rubber, which came from a rubber tree in the Congo of Africa, mixed with seed oil from Indonesia and pumice from Italy. The wood is painted yellow, from a glossy lacquer made of castor oil that came from a plant grown in India.

It literally took thousands of people to get a single pencil made and available to you at your local store. These thousands of people will probably never know or see one another, yet they are all bound by the unity of working towards a common goal. They don't speak the same language or live in the same environment, yet they are dependent on one another.

## We Need Each Other

In this modern era, we often think we are self-sufficient and we think of ourselves as individuals. We often view ourselves as independent, unique, different, and unbound by the actions and decision of others. That couldn't be further from the truth.

People have had to rely on other people since the beginning of time. This holds true for relationships as well as things. If you have a job, it's because someone hired you. If you have a family, it's because you found a partner or chose to create a life with others. In short, no one does anything alone.

There is not a single thing or person in existence that does not depend on others to exist. Even our thoughts are born of others' thoughts. Without language, there is no thought. Someone had to invent language too. It is impossible to exist without being connected to the history of humanity.

Every person we come in contact with is a wisdom teacher who knows something that we do not know and each interaction can make our lives richer. There are over 130 million books in the world right now, crammed with information, containing different opinions, perspectives, and philosophies. No one person can hold all this knowledge, therefore those holding different scopes of knowledge add to the whole.

Buddhists say we are connected to all beings, not just humans. On a scientific level that is clearly true. We are all made up of different combinations of the same building blocks of life— carbon, nitrogen, hydrogen, oxygen. Therefore, we are quite literally, all related.

The diversity of life on earth is absolutely captivating. There are more than a million and a half species that we know of and many waiting to be discovered. There are around a half-million species of plants alone. The world is filled with natural wonders, extraordinary places, and things to see that will enrich our lives and that of our children, friends, and family. They are all microcosms of the larger world we inhabit. We must be compassionate to the state of all beings and things that exist on our beautiful planet.

## Compassion in Spiritual Traditions

I am always moved when I look at the paintings by the old masters who painted golden haloes around The Madonna and other religious figures. You find the same haloes around the divine figures in all traditions, from Hindu gods to Buddhist bodhisattvas. To me, they express intellectual light combined with infinite love. Sometimes we need art, ancient and modern, to help us think in more inclusive ways. When you see the same kind of golden light around Christ as you do Krishna, you begin to see that spiritual traditions have very similar meanings.

I have been so blessed to be exposed to sacred art from so many places in the world. I've drawn so much inspiration, for my life and my books, through art, colors, and nature. Inspirational art is one of the ways the masters and those who followed have shown us the embodiment of compassion. Just take a look at an image of the Madonna, St. Theresa, or Kuan Yin and you will see compassion in action. Any art that inspires your heart to open can help you feel more compassion for yourself and for others. It is another way to cultivate compassion and give up judgment. You can even ask the sacred one in the image to take your pain, anger, and fear and help free you to experience love and compassion.

Almost every religion and spiritual practice has compassion as part of its foundation, and it is truly considered a key to happiness. In Tibetan Buddhism, compassion is the core tenet and practice.

In Buddhism, which we will discuss in the following chapters, there are practices designed to cultivate our ability to be compassionate toward all beings. There are skills—that can be developed like any other kinds of skills—which can lead to self-awareness, control over our own minds, and happiness.

Now that we have looked at the idea that we are all truly interconnected, how can we apply that knowledge to our lives and a shared search for happiness? Only by going outside our immediate circle of knowledge and comfort zone can we broaden them. My hope is that the wisdom in the chapters to come will provide inspiration for your journey.

# PART TWO

# Buddhist Philosophy
# and
# Practices for Lasting Happiness

# CHAPTER 5

# My Calling to Buddhism

*"The purpose of Buddhism is not to convert people. It is to give
them the tools so that they can create greater happiness [so that]
they can be happy no matter what their religion."*
— *Dalai Lama*

BEFORE DIVING INTO THE TOPIC of Buddhism, it is appropriate to acknowledge the person who was my original teacher and guide — Geshe Lobsang Tenzin Negi, PhD. He continues to be my one of my closest friends and spiritual brother. I have a photo of him holding my twin babies when they were three months old. He and I go way back. I still address him with a term of reverence and affection, Geshe-La, but will refer to him here as Dr. Negi.

He was born in a small Himalayan region that is adjoined by Tibet. He began his training to be a monk at the Drepung Loseling Monastery, which is in south India now, and was conferred with a Geshe Lharampa degree. This is the highest academic degree granted in the Tibetan Buddhist tradition. When we met, he was head of the monastery in Atlanta, Georgia, which serves as the North American seat. Drepung Loseling Monastery was originally founded in Tibet in 1416, but was relocated to India in the 1960s due to the Chinese Communist takeover of Tibet in 1959. In the late nineties he came to my home with ten monks who were here in the states to share their traditions with our western world. Each year, he has brought different groups of monks to my home for intensive meditation, spiritual education, and cultural exchange.

He received his PhD from Emory University in 1999 and is currently Professor of Pedagogy in Emory University's Department of Religion. He is also Executive Director of the Center for Contemplative Science and Compassion-Based Ethics, a multi-dimensional initiative, founded in 1998 as the Emory-Tibet Partnership, to bring together the foremost contributions of the Western scholastic tradition and the Tibetan Buddhist sciences of mind and healing. The Dalai Lama, who is respectfully referred to as His Holiness, had this vision that when science and spirituality come together there will be major breakthroughs and our minds will work differently, so he guided Dr. Negi to establish this program and personally inaugurated it at Emory. Through this exchange program, monks teach some of the great minds in science how to meditate—including taking them to Dharamsala where they work with His Holiness. And then, they bring some of these brilliant monks to the USA to learn science. I will share more about this in the chapter on "Buddhism and Science."

Dr. Negi has since left the monkhood but still serves as the spiritual director of the monastery in Atlanta, as well as professor and program head at Emory, and we continue to work together in a number of ways. He was the first one to expose me to meditation and Tibetan Buddhism, and I will do my best to share what I have learned over the years from him and many other Buddhist teachers who have touched my life. It's appropriate to also mention my friend Tony Tognucci, who has played an integral role in explaining the cultural nuances and intricacies of Buddhism. He has been a patient guide and teacher for over 30 years. His wisdom and insights have helped me gain in-depth understanding of Tibetan Buddhist Philosophy.

## Buddhism 101

I have admittedly been most drawn to the path of Tibetan Buddhism, which is one branch of Buddhism. But all the varieties of Buddhism have core values in common and they all have an origin story that is honored by each branch. Buddhism began with what seems like a fairy tale, but this is no fairy tale, and at least in one important way, it is the opposite of the kinds of stories we weave our fairy tales around in the west.

Our stories often start with someone who has nothing and then gains the whole world. We have the classic Rocky series, in which Rocky Balboa starts with nothing and finishes as the world champion. Or we have Cinderella, who starts with nothing as a servant of a wicked stepmother and eventually becomes a princess. But the story of Buddhism starts with a real prince who has everything and decides to give it all away.

His name is Siddhartha Gautama. He is also known as Sakyamuni, which means the Sage of the Sakya Clan. The story occurs during the fifth through sixth centuries BC, which is often called the Axial Age of Greatness, when Confucius was alive and when the Greek philosophers were flourishing. In this story the place is called Lumbini, which is the equivalent of the Buddhist version of Bethlehem. It is located in the foothills of the Himalayas in what is now Southern Nepal. The prince's mother died just a few days after Siddhartha was born, so like Confucius and Mohammad, he lost a parent as a little boy.

As a prince, he has a beautiful house, wife, and son, and a privileged life. But all of this cannot stop important questions about life and the world outside the palace from bubbling up. Soon, Siddhartha ventures from the palace to see what is going on in the outside world. Among other things he meets sick people, old people and even observes a corpse being taken to a funeral pyre. His charioteer, who was his companion, informed him that these are fates none of us can escape. We are all subject to sickness, old age, and finally death, said the charioteer. The prince was saddened by these realities.

He also met a wandering holy man, an ascetic—one who practices severe self-discipline and abstention—who had left his family, home, and job behind to go in search of spiritual liberation. Siddhartha was moved by the suffering of the world and deeply inspired by the serenity of the holy man. He decided that he too must embrace asceticism, become a wandering holy man, and find the solution to all the suffering in the world.

At the age of 29, he left everything behind and went forth in what today is called the Great Departure.

He spent six years searching. He starved himself during his strict adherence to asceticism. But in spite of being trained by some of the finest masters of that time and accomplishing many things, he was still no closer to the solution for suffering. Deciding that the path he was following would not lead him to enlightenment, he abandoned it. He selected the middle path between asceticism and hedonism (the path of satisfying one's desires).

As the story goes, he was 35 when he sat under a sacred tree (often referred to as The Bodhi Tree) in Bodhi Gaya, in northern India, determined to stay put and keep meditating until he could find a solution to suffering. Not long after that, at the dawn of a full moon known as Vaishakh Purmina, he experienced a profound awakening. He saw that all things are interconnected, impermanent, and ever-changing and that we suffer because we wish the world was otherwise. From that point forward he is known as the Buddha, the Awakened One.

When he entered onto the path as a religious leader in ancient India, it was not to claim credit for creating a movement that became known as Buddhism. He realized that he had reached enlightenment by his own effort, on his own merit, through his own experience. At first he wondered how he could convey the profound experience of enlightenment and awakening. He had no way to put it into words for others, and therefore he decided to wander in the wilderness to contemplate this for some time. After 49 days, he traveled to Deer Park in northern India to deliver his first sermon to five people who had been on the original path with him when he was an ascetic. After that teaching, known as the First Turning of the Wheel of Dharma, the five decided to join him as part of his Sangha, which translates as his community, a monastic order of monks, nuns, laymen, and lay women. And so the Buddhist mission began.

For the next forty-five years, the Buddha wandered through India teaching what he had learned. Over time, certain tenets and principles emerged in his teaching, but his primary message was: you can solve the human dilemma on your own, without recourse to divine revelation.

Eventually, Buddhism spread across Asia, and it was adapted to existing philosophies and modified in each country, accounting for the large number of variations we have today. Ideas became modified to each culture as they spread through various periods and geographical locations, but they all have the same essential contents.

## Buddhism in All Forms

Buddhists believe in the basic dignity of all human beings. They believe in the humanistic possibilities of civic morality. Their beliefs are punctuated with non-violence, gentleness, and tolerance for all and all truthfulness.

All different forms of Buddhism fall into three basic categories.

**THERAVADA.** The original and earliest form of Buddhism is called Theravada, "the way of the elders," and carries the Buddha's original message that individuals can escape suffering by learning the truth of change and not becoming attached to external things. Buddhists, as well as most Asian philosophies and religions, believe in reincarnation. In Theravada, a practitioner's primary focus is personal liberation from Samsara or the cycle of death and rebirth. This state, also known as Nirvana, is a state of lasting peace, resulting from extinguishing the inner fires of afflictive emotions such as greed, hatred and ignorance. Theravada is most popular in Thailand, Myanmar, Sri Lanka, and Cambodia.

**MAHAYANA.** The next variation is called Mahayana, "the great vehicle." This tradition of Buddhism is referred to as "the great vehicle" because of its focus on great compassion and commitment to help all beings attain freedom from their suffering. This altruistic commitment is represented in the bodhisattva ideal. Out of his or her unconditional love and compassion for all beings, the bodhisattva seeks full enlightenment or Buddhahood to help all beings in the most effective ways. In earlier forms of Buddhism, each person strives for individual liberation, but in Mahayana the emphasis is on helping others. It centers on the connectedness of all beings. Mahayana Buddhist practitioners often take the bodhisattva vow, promising that even when they are enlightened, they will come back again and again to help others. Mahayana is prevalent in China, Japan, and India.

**VAJRAYANA.** The third variation is called Vajrayana, "the diamond vehicle." This is the predominant form of Buddhism in Tibet but also has adherents in Mongolia, Bhutan, Nepal, and Russia, parts of China and Japan, and of course, India. That is where the Dalai Lama lives in exile with many of his followers today. In my own personal opinion, the epitome of Buddhist Philosophy flowers with Vajrayana. Tibetan Buddhists study all three forms of Buddhism (Theravada, Mahayana and of course Vajrayana), and to me, their philosophies, their meditations, and their education is the crowning glory of Buddhist scholarship. I will share more about this in the following sections.

## Monks Are the Teachers

Many Buddhist monks are highly educated, but in my opinion none more than the Vajrayana Buddhist monks. They study the entire Buddhist canon comprising all three traditions. Some of the most educated among them, the Geshes, those with Buddhist philosophy degrees that can take over twenty years of study and practice to attain, can quote from memory vast amounts of the scriptures. They engage in critical inquiry, utilizing advanced forms of logic and debate.

The Tibetans have many accomplishments, all of which have become part of their Buddhist traditions. Tibetan medicine is one of the most effective forms of medicine on the planet. The Tibetan sacred arts are unparalleled anywhere else in the world. The Tibetans have a very long history, beginning before modern religions and reaching back to shamanic times. Many of those indigenous cultural elements and practices have been incorporated into Vajrayana Buddhism, and these rituals play a very important part in their traditions.

Tibetan Buddhist monks, nuns, and practitioners are also trained in mystical arts, rituals and meditations. One of the most recognizable art forms to Westerners is the sand mandala. A mandala is not simply a work of art or a picture of something. Each mandala in this tradition is a roadmap to enlightenment in highly symbolic form. The artistic skill and training required to construct a sand mandala is amazing in and of itself. Teams of monks work simultaneously for many hours at a time to create the mandalas by placing individual grains of colored sand in intricate patterns by hand, using a metal funnel called chak phur. It requires the utmost focus and concentration, which is held for hours over multiple days. The monks are not simply creating by rote; they must understand the spiritual meaning behind every symbol in the mandala, which is considered a roadmap to enlightenment. This would be an incredible feat for even one mandala, but most of these monks are trained in about a dozen mandalas, in different versions. Spreading blessings and messages of peace are central themes of Buddhism, and there are many symbolic representations of it.

Another important symbol is Tibetan prayer flags. The flags blow and flap in the breeze, sending the blessing written on them into the wind to be spread over the earth. There are also large metal cylinders inscribed with Tibetan prayers that the monks turn by hand and which have been featured in films, such as "Seven Years in Tibet." These are called prayer wheels, and again, the idea is that the blessings inscribed on those cylinders will be spread throughout the land as they are turned by the monks. The goal of the monks is not only to do good things that are for the benefit of others, but also to make sure that nothing is done that may cause harm.

Because the main tenet in Buddhism teaches that everything is impermanent, after they build the sand mandalas, following days and days of labor and intense concentration, they dismantle the mandala and sweep it into piles of multicolored sand. They don't get attached to their artwork and don't frame or preserve it for posterity. They destroy it because non-attachment to the things of the world is a core Buddhist principle.

As part of the closing ceremony for the destruction of the mandalas, the monks put some of the sand from the mandala into small envelopes and give it away so people can carry those blessing away into their lives. Then they take the rest of the sand and scoop it into a beautiful ritual vase. The traditional ceremony continues with a procession to a river or any nearby open body of water where they scatter the sand into the water which, like the prayer flags and prayer wheels, now spread the blessings throughout the land. This water also evaporates into the sky and falls back again, raining blessings on the earth, bestowing upon all the great gift of peace. It is a beautiful sight to behold.

## Buddhism Does Not Demand Worship

Buddhism does not believe that it is the "one and only true religion," nor does it suggest that tradition will last forever. They believe in the philosophy of impermanence, so ideas in Buddhism are not fixed and unchangeable. To this day, thousands of monks debate the idea of Buddhism and are willing to change their ideas if a convincing argument is proposed that makes any of their principles seem incorrect. Personally, I find the openness and flexibility profound and beautiful.

Unlike some religions, Buddhism does not want you to have blind faith. The Buddha taught that you must never follow someone simply because that person claims to know the truth, but that you must learn the truth for yourself. Thus, blind faith is not required. In that sense Buddhism is more like a science than a religion. It considers empirical evidence as the foremost authority, yet also reminds us that, as Dr. Negi would say, "The absence of evidence is not the evidence for its absence."

The Buddha put it this way: "Monks and scholars, just as a goldsmith would test his gold by burning, cutting, and polishing it, so you must examine my words and accept them, but not merely out of respect for me."

# CHAPTER 6

# The Buddha Offered an Approach to Life

*"Buddha was a unique psychotherapist. His therapeutic methods helped millions of people throughout the centuries."*
— *Tapas Kumar Aich*

The simple version of what the Buddha taught was:

1. Everything has the potential to cause suffering.
2. Suffering is caused primarily by what we think and believe.
3. Since suffering has a cause, and the cause is identified, suffering can be cured.
4. Then he relayed *how* to do it.

## Four Noble Truths

He set forth these four principles, which are known as the "Four Noble Truths."

- The First Noble Truth explains what may seem obvious: Life contains many possibilities for suffering. Whatever we have that is good can be lost. Possessions are lost, health wanes, and everyone dies someday. Every living creature is subject to those same things.
- The Buddha said most of our suffering is not caused directly by the things that happen, but by what we think about those things. Dr. Negi has said, "Pain is inevitable, but suffering

is a choice." This is the Second Noble Truth.

- The Third Noble Truth says that since the source of our suffering lies in our mental states and actions, we can learn to change our perceptions and reactions and greatly diminish, or even eliminate, suffering.
- The Fourth Noble Truth teaches the techniques to accomplish this goal through cultivating mindfulness, wisdom, and an ethical lifestyle. Meditation helps to achieve these inner skills.

## The Eightfold Path

The Eightfold Path is among the most well-known foundations of early Buddhist tradition. This foundational Buddhist model consists of eight principles to live by. These appeared in *The Pāli Canon*, which contains some of the most ancient aspects of Buddhist scripture. Writing for *Tricycle Magazine*, Walpola Sri Rahula described them as "The Buddha's practical instructions to reach the end of suffering." They are:

1. Right understanding (*Samma ditthi)*
2. Right thought (*Samma sankappa*)
3. Right speech (*Samma vaca*)
4. Right action (*Samma kammanta*)
5. Right livelihood (*Samma ajiva*)
6. Right effort (*Samma vayama*)
7. Right mindfulness (*Samma sati*)
8. Right concentration (*Samma samadhi*)

## Some Basic Buddhist Concepts

Buddhist teachings come in two forms: theory and practice.

Although Buddhism doesn't require blind faith, it insists you examine any teachings or concepts and draw conclusions for yourself. This begins with awareness and understanding of suffering, how it is self-imposed, and how it can be eliminated.

## Dependent Arising

The first part of the theory is explained in the Buddhist philosophy by two interrelated ideas called dependent arising and emptiness. Dependent arising suggests that everything arises and is dependent on something else to exist.

And emptiness, from the Buddhist perspective, refers to a state of being that is devoid of fixed, concrete, or independent status. In other words, dependent arising and emptiness are two sides of the same coin. That is, any given thing or event comes to exist independent upon various contributing factors and therefore is empty of having fixed and independent nature. In the Buddhist tradition, failing to recognize this reality is at the very root of all our suffering. This manifests in various forms of our mental projections that are not grounded in reality.

Let me illustrate with a couple of stories.

Dependent arising theory states that when a sentient being and *something else* meet, another thing is created. This is a product of their interaction and is not contained in either thing, in and of itself. Suffering is created by our own prejudice and perception.

For example, suppose you have a little boy named Matthew who discovers a box of crayons lying on the coffee table. He decides to give you a special gift of a drawing—on your newly painted living room wall. Suppose he is well into his masterpiece before you come in from the kitchen and notice him scribbling on the wall like crazy. How would you feel at that moment? Excited for his artistic talents and intention to draw you a mural? Or very upset? Furious? Even filled with despair because you used your last paycheck to have the wall painted?

Being upset is a normal reaction. You are not a bad parent for feeling stressed about your wall. But, if you step back from the situation, you may find that your child has not truly betrayed you—he wanted to make you a drawing. And the wall has not offended you. But somehow, you have *allowed* the drawing on the wall to be the source of great pain. The negative thoughts and emotional suffering you are feeling are the result of your thoughts *about* the crayoned wall. It's not truly the end of the world, but your perception is that the drawing is causing you pain.

The drawing didn't create those feelings. You felt badly because of your own perspective and opinion about such things. In essence, you just chose suffering. You may think that the drawing on the wall justifies your feelings, but from the Buddhist perspective, your feelings are not absolutely necessary. The issue is not the thing itself; it is how you deal with it.

Shift perspective for a moment through the eyes of your child. Matthew saw the same marks and thought they were pretty cool.

Here's another story to consider:

Three people are walking in the woods. As they pass under a tree, a snake falls and lands in front of them.

- The first person is a man who lives in the city. Because he has never seen a living snake before, he is totally freaked out and begins running for his life.
- The second person was once in the military. He was taught that there are only five types of deadly poisonous snakes in the area and the others pose no immediate danger. He also knows from his experience that this particular snake is *not* poisonous, so he has no concern and feels nothing.
- The third person is a herpetologist. She is well versed in snakes and other reptiles. She knows immediately that this snake is rare. She has never seen one before in her studies. She is ecstatic, imagining all the accolades and advancement this will bring to her career.

Here we have three people in the same place, at the same time, and they are encountering the same snake. One is frightened, one feels nothing, and one is excited. The theory of dependent arising says that fear, boredom, or bliss are the result of what qualities we attribute to the object; meaning those qualities are not inherent attributes. It is the combination of the snake and the individual perceptions of the three witnesses that cause those feelings to arise.

This philosophy of emptiness is often translated into English in a negative way, to mean nothingness or a void. But this is not the same meaning that Buddhism has in mind. From the Buddhist perspective, the snake by itself cannot cause fear, boredom, or bliss. The emotional reaction is dependent on both the snake's existence and the perception of another being.

To put it simply, the dependent arising doctrine is essentially saying that you construct the emotional content of the world in your own mind. You need to see for yourself the prejudices you live with and how they may add suffering. This is the only way you can begin to change them.

## Impermanence and Interconnectedness

Buddhists define compassion as "The wish to help free others from dissatisfaction or suffering." Love is defined as "the wish to give happiness to others." Buddhists strive to remove suffering and give happiness.

To achieve happiness, Buddhists rely on two philosophical ideas: impermanence and interconnectedness.

The doctrine of impermanence says that nothing will last forever. You will eventually die, and when you do, your wealth, friends, and status will not be taken with you. Mountains will eventually wear down, and oceans dry up. Since all things are constantly changing, you cannot count on them for happiness.

The concept of interconnectedness tells us that we do not exist in a vacuum as individuals. The world and everyone in it are intrinsically linked.

The Buddhists sometimes call their teachings the "sacred secret of happiness." The highest teaching of all Mahayana Buddhists, including Tibetan monks, is the desire to do everything for the benefit of all beings. This desire to fully commit to the other's well-being arises from the profound understanding that we are all interconnected. A point His Holiness the Dalai Lama often makes is that there is great urgency in recognizing the oneness of humanity.

## How Do We Change?

The core belief in Buddhism is that you must think for yourself. This means we must strive to sort out the *reality* of each moment from the ways in which we *interpret* reality. We tend to see the world around us through the lens of our own assumptions and our distorted perceptions. I believe we can achieve a more realistic understanding of life and the world we live in through meditation.

There are many different types of meditations, and many ways in which it is taught. Here are two that I find helpful dealing with emotionally difficult thoughts.

CALM ABIDING MEDITATION. This is an exercise to see the scattered nature of your mind and sow the seeds to stabilize it. It is a form of mindfulness, which means simply paying attention to the present moment without judgment. Humans innately grasp for meaning through their thoughts, often holding on to unhealthy ideas. Buddhists call it "attachment." As a thought enters the mind, we engage with it and absorb ourselves in it, even if it causes pain—and we keep returning to these hurtful thoughts. This prevents us from discovering our own true nature, which is pure and compassionate. It prevents us from living in the here and now. Calm abiding meditation can help you get centered.

INSIGHT MEDITATION. This cultivates critical thinking about your own personal philosophies and what they mean in everyday life. Insight meditation allows reflection on negative emotions and behaviors, and how they create suffering. It helps you discover some of the ways you are not helpful to yourself or others. For example:

- Lies you tell yourself
- Feelings of anger that you show others
- Negative traits you may have
- Ways in which you withhold love from yourself or others
- Feeling unworthy or undeserving
- Feeling resentful
- Feeling like a victim

Without judgment, without dwelling on what you think is bad in yourself, seeing how these negative things harm you will lead to their end.

These two types of practices help us come to "realizations," which in Buddhist terminology means that we understand something in such a way that it forever changes our lives. Through meditation our oneness becomes apparent. Our desire to be happy and how we can accomplish that will gain clarity because we understand that it is a product of our perceptions. We can then meditate to transform our perceptions and go from a place of judgment to a place of observation without judgment, and then to a place of self-love and love for all beings. This process of first recognizing facts, and then analyzing without judgment, can be applied to aspects of our everyday life with great success.

After developing a regular meditation practice, we begin to see the interconnectedness of all things, and this brings us to the core values of Buddhism: love and compassion.

## Self-Love and Love for Others

The very first lesson the Buddha taught was that we cause our own happiness or suffering depending on our own attitudes and actions. If we are not kind or loving to others, we create the conditions that could prevent us from leading a good life. That is why it is so important to find a way to wish everyone happiness, even if we don't think they deserve it.

Buddhist philosophy also teaches that you have to love

yourself in order to love others, so you want to cultivate your authentic self.

The following chapters explain some of the Buddhist meditations, exercises, and approaches that can help you practice compassion and love.

## CHAPTER 7

# Embracing the Four Virtues of the Heart
# Virtues One and Two

*"Until you have real compassion, you cannot recognize love."*
*— Bob Thurman*

THE HEART HAS A VERY special place in Tibetan Buddhism. It fosters such things as friendliness, compassion, empathy, and sympathy. Of all these types of virtues, there are four very special ones which, according to Tibetan teachings, abide in the heart.

Sometimes they are simply called "the Four Virtues of the Heart," but they have other names as well, such as:

- The Four Immeasurables
- The Four Perfect Virtues
- The Brahma-viharas (abodes of Brahma)
- The Sublime Attitudes
- The Four Divine States of Dwelling
- The Four Divine Abodes
- The Four Bhavanas

These qualities are also considered four states of mind that interrelate and strengthen each other. Buddha taught these virtues to his followers, and they have been passed along over the ages. Buddhists today often access and cultivate these virtues through meditation.

In fact, the Sanskrit word for meditation, Bhavana, can be translated as "the cultivation of," so each of the four Bhavanas I am sharing here is used to cultivate one of the Four Virtues of the Heart.

## How Do They Help Us?

The virtues of the heart are all qualities that are extremely beneficial to develop because they aim to open the heart. One way to know ourselves is to know our own hearts, and these four virtues can help us do so. Developing these virtues can give you "a heart that knows no bounds." As an interesting aside, science has shown that when someone practices compassion their heart is literally affected. Studies have shown that compassion lowers the risk of heart disease by boosting the positive effects of the vagus nerve, which helps to slow our heart rate. It is also great for our brains! Matthieu Ricard, a Buddhist monk and writer who has been the subject of scientific investigation, led to the discovery that an area of the brain lights up during meditation. As a very advanced meditator, he submitted to brain scans, and in many international news stories it was said he had the greatest capacity for happiness ever recorded. He was called "the happiest man alive." When asked what he was meditating on, he said "compassion."

On a practical level, the Four Virtues of the Heart can only help us live happier, kinder, and more balanced lives. The virtues are:

- Loving-kindness or benevolence (Metta)
- Compassion (Karuna)
- Empathetic joy (Mudita)
- Equanimity (Upekkha)

In this chapter and the next we will look deeply into the meaning of these four virtues and discuss each component. In the section on meditations and exercises in the back of this book, you will find a powerful "Metta Meditation" to give you a way to enact these virtues and include them in your meditation practice.

## The First Virtue of the Heart (Metta Bhavana)
## Cultivating Loving-Kindness

The word Metta is a Pali word similar to the Sanskrit word, Maitri. It translates as "love" and also means benevolence, friendliness, amity, good will, loving-kindness, and active interest in others. Some people may even describe it as "preferring welfare" or "removal of annoyance." Some people consider this word to mean friendliness or being a friendly person. I like to look at it from the more classical Buddhist interpretation of "the cultivation of loving-kindness."

But in the case of Metta Bhavana, love is used differently from how we perceive that word in our daily lives. The word "love" tends to have a very strong romantic emotional aspect; in this context it is *not* that kind of emotion. In essence, love is seen as a context in which our hearts and minds should dwell. It is an attitude we want to cultivate and have with us at all times and in all circumstances.

In other disciplines of meditation, people often do inner work or exercises and then get back to their normal living. In Buddhist philosophy, meditation is never just an exercise we do for a certain number of minutes and then go on with our daily lives. The whole point of any and all Buddhist meditation is to *change* our minds and mental attitudes. The goal is to cultivate various virtues so that they will be with us throughout our lives, in every circumstance, enabling us to meet life with new skills, abilities, and resiliency. Every exercise or meditation here is meant to be entirely practical.

All Buddhist philosophy begins with the essential axiom that all people want to be happy. This is often described as "living with ease." So, to put it in its simplest terms, in the cultivation of loving-kindness you simply wish for others to be happy as well.

# The Second Virtue of the Heart
# (Karuna Bhavana)
# Cultivating Compassion

The word Karuna translates as compassion and can also refer to self-compassion. Through the second virtue of the heart we care about the suffering of others. This is truly a core value of the philosophy of the Buddha. Initially, what started him on his path was that he saw sickness, old age, and death all around him and he witnessed suffering of all kinds. He resolved to solve the problem of suffering.

Once he became the Buddha (enlightened one), he was asked the question: "What is it that you teach?" He answered: "All that I teach are two things: there is dukkha and the end of dukkha." The word "dukkha" that he used is usually translated as suffering, but can actually mean anything that you find *unsatisfactory.*

In the Metta Bhavana, we focus on wishing happiness and health for others. In the Karuna Bhavana, we begin by focusing on heartfelt wishes for others to be free from suffering.

## Karuna Bhavana

Sit comfortably and start with calming and centering by taking a few deep breaths and relaxing. Then consciously think about what you are about to do so that you can do it mindfully. In this case, we remind ourselves that we are trying to cultivate one of the virtues of the heart in which we simply wish good things to whomever we focus on during the exercise. We simply wish that they can be free from suffering and its causes. This can be repeated over and over again, for numerous intended recipients.

### Exercise 1: Choose a Benefactor for Your Good Wishes

Start by thinking of someone who is a positive person in your life. This can be a family member or someone you love, a good friend, or an individual you admire.

Let's refer to this person who is the recipient of your wish as a benefactor. There are many ways for a person to be a benefactor. It could be someone who has been generous to you, with their time, wisdom, or money. It could be someone who regularly comforts you, cares for you, or guides you with their compassionate words. It could even be someone you don't know personally, but who has inspired you from afar; perhaps the author of a book that touched you deeply, or a wise person in the public eye who has been a role model or inspired you in some way.

For this exercise, it should be someone that you know is suffering in some way. Maybe they are dealing with illness, loss, a recent accident, or unemployment. Perhaps they are caregiving for a sick or elderly loved one, or their family is in financial trouble and it is causing them to suffer. Whatever kind of hard time they are in, you want to send your good thoughts. But you also want to do this in a grounded and unemotional way, so that you do not open yourself to taking on their suffering and so that you do not try to fix it for them.

Bring that person to mind and call gentle focus on the situation of their suffering. Picture them in your mind in the most positive, whole, and healed way.

Now say something like:

**May you be free from suffering and the causes of suffering.**

Once you have finished with this person, it's time to move on to the next person. In theory you can extend your compassion and cultivate this wish for all beings. In the infinitely connected world of existence, everyone is contributing to our needs directly or indirectly, intentionally and unintentionally, and is therefore a benefactor. This level of compassion is what the Buddhists call "great compassion." If you are on a roll, you can do many people at once. You can also choose to do one a day for as many days as you feel you can to develop this as an ongoing practice.

## Exercise 2: Choosing Yourself as Benefactor of Your Good Wishes

Now give yourself the same loving compassion you offered to those people you care about. You are entitled to be your own benefactor and to give yourself the good wishes you have offered to others.

Think about the good things you have done in your life. Think of the ways you have been open to learning, healing, and giving to others. Know that each and every person who strives for happiness and kindness is making this world a better place. Now be your own best friend and offer yourself Karuna Bhavana by thinking of something that troubles you. Allow an image of yourself in your mind from a happier and calmer time. And say the following:

**May I be free from suffering and from the causes of suffering.**

Focus on you and your good qualities, and then extend good wishes to yourself.

Do this for yourself often. As you progress in these cultivations, you will become more and more of a benefactor to both yourself and others. When you give to another, remember to also take time to make yourself a benefactor as well.

The second virtue reminds us that all of us have something "dissatisfactory" in our lives. We all have friends who are sick, suffering, or having problems, and to some extent we suffer too when people we care about are not doing well. Not to mention, we all have our own problems. Life may be good, but it is not trouble-free.

Practicing Virtues One and Two prepares us for the third. Take a deep breath and continue on to the next chapter.

## CHAPTER 8

# Embracing the Four Virtues of the Heart
# Virtues Three and Four

*"Love and kindness are never wasted. They always make a
difference. They bless the one who receives them,
and they bless you, the giver."*
— Barbara De Angelis

Now you are ready to explore the third and fourth Virtues of the
Heart.

## The Third Virtue of the Heart (Mudita Bhavana)
## Cultivating Empathic Joy

IN SOME WAYS THIS IS the simplest of the cultivations. With
this virtue we simply rejoice in the well-being of others. This
counteracts jealousy and resentment over the good fortune of
others.

1.  Start with yourself. Consider all the things you are grateful
    for. Think of all the things that bring joy to your life. Then
    utter these phrases to state your intentions. For example:

    **I am grateful for the goodness and joy in my life.**
    **May I continue to be joyful.**

**May the causes of my joy continue.**

2. Then move on to a friend, benefactor, or someone you love or admire. You might consider someone who seems to be joyous all the time. I have a friend like that, and you may also. The Dalai Lama is a very good example of such a person. Bring a person like that to mind and reflect on the kind of life they lead and all the qualities you admire. Try to share in that joy. Then utter the same phrases.

**May you be grateful for the goodness and joy in your life.**
**May you continue to be joyful.**
**May the causes of your joy continue.**

3. Next, utter these same phrases in honor of a neutral person.

4. Then, extend those same kind words to a difficult person.

5. As usual, we end with wishes for all beings. When I do this exercise, I visualize the whole globe. You can try that, or whatever works for you. There is great power in including so many different people and perspectives in this exercise. Here's why:

- **THE POWER OF FOCUSING ON OURSELVES.** This is an especially useful exercise when applied to *you* as the person of focus. This is not in order to falsely build up your ego and have you convince yourself that you are the most fabulous person on the planet. But since many of us have spent a considerable portion of our lives berating ourselves for our shortcomings (real or imagined), it is good to remember that *all* people have some good qualities. So think of your own virtues and rejoice in them.

- **THE POWER OF FOCUSING ON A JOYOUS FRIEND.** One of the things that I've noticed about my perpetually joyous friend is that she engages in conversation with *everyone* she meets and asks them about their families, their jobs, and so on. She truly treats all people as equals and looks down on no one. Of course, there is a secret to this as well: My friend isn't nice to people because she is following some script to benefit herself. She actually *enjoys* other people and *wants* to know about them. This type of behavior will bring joy to others and to you. The more awake you are, the more you can cultivate joy in all conditions.

- **THE POWER OF FOCUSING ON A NEUTRAL PERSON.** This would be someone whom you have no particular opinion about or whom perhaps you simply do not know well. At first glance, a neutral person is someone you are indifferent to. Looking at this further, we see that the "neutral" person is somebody you are indifferent to because you don't think about them or notice them much. In the coldest sense, they don't seem to affect your life much, so you don't invest time in them.

Focusing on neutral people helps us avoid an error on several levels. Remember when we talked about how (virtually) everything you see, everything you own, and so on, was provided by someone else? This means nobody is really neutral because at some level we receive a benefit from every human being. In addition, we are trying to develop the virtues of the heart, which means we are learning to offer our hearts to all. We should not be indifferent to anybody. And if you practice mindfulness and learn a little something about this so-called neutral person, you will find that there is always something valuable or at least enjoyable to learn about them or from them. We simply have not noticed. Practicing mindfulness is all about noticing; it makes the invisible visible. So learn to look in the eyes of the neutral person and make them visible. Humans long to be seen. Showing any interest in a person will make them happier, and giving them attention will also make you happier. I am convinced that formulating a connection to other people makes all of us happier people.

- **THE POWER OF FOCUSING ON A DIFFICULT PERSON.** You may not like someone's attitude or politics, and you may even bristle over their behavior and prejudices, but still, you can rise above that and practice sending compassion and empathic joy to all. It may help to realize that they act the way they do because they are hurt, scared, or traumatized by something that happened in their lives. Focusing on the negativity breeds more negativity. Focusing on compassion and kindness plants a seed for possibility. This seed may not grow in the heart of the troublesome person, but at least you have used your compassion in a productive and helpful way. The more people who can do this, the more compassionate our world will become.

In summary, it is our natural habit (because of how the unconscious works) to see things and immediately judge them: Dangerous, important, insignificant, and so on. Mindfulness weakens the link between bare perception and automatic judgments. *Mudita Bhavana* is an exercise that is used not to sympathize with the joy of others, but to celebrate their virtues. We think of their virtues and we rejoice in them.

We start our exercises with somebody we like, and we progress to end with someone we dislike before we offer it to "all beings." The neutral person then, is someone in between those two extremes. It might include a salesperson, or a cashier, or a waitress, or somebody you sit next to in a class, an office, or on a train.

When you can learn to see what is hidden, even a walk down a street you have traveled on countless times will show you endless things to appreciate and enjoy. Some say this demonstrates that mindfulness is a miracle; I say that since you are just seeing what was already there, it proves that *the world* is a miracle!

## The Fourth Virtue of the Heart
## (Upekkha Bhavana)
## Cultivating Equanimity

Equanimity has many different definitions, but here it is primarily interpreted as impartiality. It is one of the core values of Buddhist philosophy.

We have focused on ourselves, people we like, and people we perceive are neutral. Most of us want happiness for ourselves and our loved ones. And while we may not naturally have warmth or love for neutral people, we don't feel anything negative toward them. It is not hard to include them in our well-wishes. But we have a tendency to be hostile towards those who are hostile to us, or those whose conduct we think is reprehensible. These people would be considered the difficult persons.

The hero of the Tibetan Buddhist world is called a bodhisattva—someone who vows to obtain enlightenment to use it in the service of all beings. One of the reasons that the virtues of the heart are called immeasurable or boundless is that they have no limits. They are not only for a small group of special people but for *all beings*. So in this philosophy, to truly develop equanimity, to make these virtues truly immeasurable or boundless, you can't only offer them to friends or loved ones. And you cannot superimpose boundaries on what you are offering. These practices are meant to help us develop a heart that knows no bounds, and thus they must be offered to all.

For those of you who are religious, think of it this way: Does your God love only certain people, or all people? If you are a Christian you may remember that when Jesus was asked what was the most important commandment or practice, an important part of his answer was, "Thou shalt love thy neighbor as thyself." Even Jesus assumed that you should love yourself, but when he advised you to love others, he didn't say that you should love only the nice ones, but all of them.

In Buddhist philosophy, it is believed that we all have a Buddha nature. When Siddhartha understood suffering, its sources, and its cure, he decided that we are born pristine and that we all have a flawless center. But then we start to build a personality, which is an idea that separates *me* from *you* (and all else). This, he believed, makes our minds become clouded and, in essence, sick. This sickness is what leads to negative emotions such as jealousy, hatred, and so on. The way that he looked at it, our minds are diseased by these divisive internal thoughts.

In the literature on the study of the brain, there is a very famous story about Phineas P. Gage who was a very pleasant person that everybody liked. One day he had an accident and a 13-pound rod went through his head and right through his brain. You would expect that he would die instantly, but he didn't. They managed to get the rod removed and he lived. You would expect that he would have little use of his brain, not know much anymore, and not be able to function well. But that didn't happen. At first it seemed there was nothing wrong. But soon everyone noticed changes in his personality. He became mean and insulting, and he uttered a constant string of profanities. But those who knew his case didn't blame him. They realized that the only reason he was acting that way was because the traumatic injury impacted the frontal lobe, the area of the brain related to personality. His case went on to make a huge contribution to neuroscience.

In much the same ways, bodhisattvas realize that the only reason people act badly is because their brain is sick and has developed the diseases of hatred, jealousy, and other negative qualities. Bodhisattvas learn to attribute the unpleasantness in people to the disease—not to the person. For example, you wouldn't be angry at a person with a disease of the nervous system that caused involuntary body twitches or uncontrolled shouting of profanities, because you would assume that the disease is responsible. You may hate the disease, but not the person. The same is true of people who have been damaged by life.

As the Buddha taught and Buddhism continues to teach, all beings have a pristine nature, but it has been clouded over by their bad experiences, by the lack of love shown to them, and by a myriad of other circumstances. There may not be a cure at hand for all the ways our nervous systems and brains become ill, but we don't help anything by attacking the person. Society's methods for dealing with mental illness, disease, and crime are not designed for healing as much as they are designed to mask problems, treat symptoms, and punish people for bad behavior. All of these things may be necessary, but they are not all transformative or rehabilitative.

Buddhist philosophy reminds us that things are changing constantly. That includes behavior. Behavior, like all other things, happens in conjunction with all sorts of dependent conditions— and those can change. In my life I have had some people who started out as adversaries or downright enemies, but later became friends and changed their behavior. So recognizing that a person can change, we at least wish for them to have a chance to change. That's why our meditation phrases are always stated in two thoughts:

**May you be happy.**
**May you be free from the causes of unhappiness.**

In this final virtue of the heart, and this final cultivation, we offer our wishes toward the difficult person and, then, toward all beings.

Of course, there are many degrees and levels of what we might call a difficult person, ranging from something minor like somebody who chews loudly and annoys you, to people at the level of the worst dictators and murderers. But let's focus for the moment on the people who annoy us or whom we may even think of as enemies, but who are *not* serial killers, child molesters, or despots engaged in genetic cleansing.

Why should you wish wellness, compassion, and joy toward

any of these difficult people? You might wonder, "What's in it for me?" and "Why should I send my good energy to that annoying person?" There are many reasons. Here are some of the most important:

- The cultivation of equanimity aids in the cultivation of all the virtues of the heart. By developing equanimity through Upekkha Bhavana, we learn to offer loving-kindness, compassion, and sympathetic joy for *all* beings. Equanimity encompasses positive wishes for all beings. When we consider that we are all interrelated, that all things are impermanent, and that we all wish for a peaceful life, we are led to embrace equanimity even more. When we understand that all human hearts hold within them the seed for understanding, we find yet another reason to embrace equanimity.

- On a practical level, life is ever-changing and fraught with events that may not always be to our liking. Tough times may make us think it is especially difficult to practice equanimity. As in many areas of life, we may think we understand something one moment, and in the next moment act as if we never understood at all. Many of us have been taught that we should love one another and that all people are equal in some sense, but how many of us actually practice that consistently? Practicing equanimity gives us a reliable way to feel like we are making a difference in some small way.

- This practice helps us expand our world. There are many reasons not to be happy with another person. Perhaps they don't feel the same way about the environment or don't have the same work ethic. But in the end, it amounts to not liking another person because they are not *you*. There is no future in disapproving of others because they are not your philosophical clones. So in that sense, developing equanimity is working toward a cure for one of the main obstacles and causes of our dissatisfactions in our lives: Being self-centered. It encourages us to love people as they are, to try to understand them where they are coming from, and to act kindly and compassionately toward them no matter who they are.

Just to be clear, we do not have magic powers to change anyone. And just because we wish for someone's happiness, it does not mean they will become happier. Our wishes, in themselves, will not bring the person instant happiness. We are all, ultimately, responsible for our own happiness, as well as our own unhappiness. Our wishes for others will not come true unless the objects of those wishes free themselves from the causes of unhappiness. However, making the effort to practice this virtue may just add magic and healing to our *own* lives because it frees us from carrying the burden of hatred.

## The Power of the Four Immeasurables

Embracing the Four Virtues is good for our souls.

Tibetan Buddhist teachers often remind us of the importance of our thoughts and deeds by sharing this popular saying, "What we are today is the result of how we have acted in the past. What we will be tomorrow is the result of what we think today." This reflects one of the Buddha's most important insights.

When we reflect on that, we see that all experience is conditioned by and preceded by our very thoughts. This should make us realize that there is no good outcome in trying to control others, in hating others, or even in having negative thoughts about others.

Offering loving-kindness, compassion, empathic joy, and equanimity to ourselves and others as a practice will change our lives and our world.

## CHAPTER 9

# The Jewel in the Lotus and Sacred Symbols

*"Every person possesses the Buddha-nature."*
*— Dogen*

THE TIBETANS HAVE MANY MEDITATIONS and exercises that focus on the heart. To work with these meditations, it is helpful to learn some of the Buddhist symbolism and to become familiar with the most popular and often evoked mantra of them all:

**Om Mani Padme Hum.**

Spoken phonetically it may sound like: *Ohm Man-ee Pad-may Hung*. It translates to "Praise to the Jewel in the Lotus."

It is a chant that every Tibetan child grows up with, taught to them by parents early in life. It is used in daily practice in meditations, prayers with mala beads, and even chanted on the way to the temple.

I've heard it chanted, sung, and hummed. Some people do it in multiples of seven, twenty-one, or 108 times. It may be included at the start or in the midst of other meditations and used as a meditation unto itself. It is often carved into Buddhist temples and structures as a blessing. And some meditations involve visualizing this mantra at your heart.

This chant often comes to Buddhists in any difficult situation.

Om Mani Padme Hum is a central prayer for Buddhists. By comparison, a Catholic might evoke the Hail Mary, and a person of the Jewish faith may chant the Shema Yisrael.

## What or Who Is the Jewel in the Lotus?

The Jewel in the Lotus has numerous interpretations.

Some schools of Buddhism say that the six syllables comprised in Om Mani Padme Hum have specific meanings. One interpretation is, "The combined practice of infinite altruism, compassion, and wisdom to transform one's impure body, speech, and mind into that of a Buddha."

Harry C. Emberson, a Kagyu Tibetan Buddhist, described it this way: "Om is a seed syllable beginning most mantras. Mani is Jewel. Peme (or Padme) is Lotus and Hung is the seed syllable used at the end of most mantras (also with esoteric meanings)."

Om Mani Padme Hum is also considered the Mantra of the God/Goddess of Compassion. Thus many people consider that it is a chant to the Buddhist Goddess Kuan Yin in one of her many forms.

She is considered a mother of mercy and the pinnacle of compassion, kindness, and love. Some legends say she was a human princess who was punished by her father when she refused to marry and who suffered terribly as a result. Now viewed as an Avalokiteshvara and bodhisattva, she is considered an enlightened being who earned the right to leave the human world of suffering but who chose to stay until the last suffering soul has been healed. She took the bodhisattva vow to rescue all beings from suffering: "By the virtues of generosity and other perfections, may I attain Enlightenment for the benefit of all beings."

She is precious and beloved in many cultures. In statues and images, she is often seen with a vase, pouring healing water onto the world, standing on a dragon or holding a baby. She is often portrayed as motherly and considered to be a nurturer who sacrificed bliss in order to save her children.

Buddhists around the world call to many different aspects of the Buddha, including those known as Avalokiteshvara. They are the ones that embody the compassion of all Buddhas. Kuan Yin is a female bodhisattva. However, this kindhearted one is also seen as male. Both are called upon in meditation, chants, prayers, and celebrations and known by many names in multiple cultures.

- Tibetans call this highest embodiment of compassion by the name Chenrezig. The name means, "One who looks with an unwavering eye." He renounced Nirvana in order to help mankind. Tibetans often refer to His Holiness the Dalai Lama by that name as they consider him to be a reincarnation of the Buddha of Compassion in human form.
- Chinese culture calls her Kuan Yin or Guan Yin, as well as several other variations of those names. Chinese Buddhists revere her as the Goddess of Mercy. The name Guanyin is short for Guanshiyin, which essentially translates into the one who perceives the sounds (or cries) of the world. Taoists also call her Guanyin Pusa and they consider her an immortal.
- In Japanese culture, she is known as a bodhisattva called Kannon. She is known for helping people who are in distress and is worshipped widely in Japanese temples.
- Korean culture calls her by several names, including: Kwanseieun and Gwan Eum. She is seen as a deity of goodness, courage and fortune who lives on this earthly plane to pay attention to our needs and resolve each with compassion.
- In India and Nepal, both Buddhist and Hindus pray to compassionate beings that carry the energy of the Avalokiteshvara. There are several names including, Padmapani, Seto Machindranath, and Janabaha Dyo.

## A Note about Buddhists and Divinity

Despite the commonly used term of Goddess of Compassion, Buddhists do not relate to the concept of God or Goddess in the same way as Westerners. To Westerners the Divine is the Supreme Being who created all there is and who is all powerful. Buddhists don't believe in that concept. They also do not consider the Buddha to be a god in the sense of a creator of the world. In the same vein, The Dalai Lama is not considered to be a god.

Buddhists pray to many different aspects of the Buddha by name, including the aspect of Avalokiteshvara that we discussed above. And they sometimes pray in temples and spiritual gatherings. Buddhist deities are usually depicted in images and statues as being seated on thrones or lotuses, representing their sacred nature. But the different Buddhas represent different qualities or virtues, rather than divinity as we know it in the West. For example, another important bodhisattva is Tara, who is considered a savioress in the Tibetan tradition. Om tare tuttare ture svaha. This mantra invokes the blessings of Tara for protection from the suffering caused by the cycle of death and rebirth, all forms of fear, and from illness. She has many aspects, comes in different shades, and is called upon for protection, healing, and enlightenment.

Medicine Buddha is another aspect of Buddha considered a healing being who soothes physical, mental, and emotional afflictions. His images are always blue. But he is not a god as much as he is a symbol of healing.

My experience is that, because of the symbolism of these deities, looking at images or statues of them is powerful because it helps us evoke the blessings and inspirations of the virtues they embody.

In Tibetan Buddhism, the Jewel in the Lotus goes beyond the concept of the Goddess or God of Compassion. It is rich with symbolism and metaphors that relate to the human condition—and how to uplift it.

## The Significance of the Lotus and the Jewel

There are a number of ways to interpret the importance and significance of the lotus and the jewel. I asked my friend Dr. Negi to explain it from the traditional Tibetan perspective. He explained it this way:

"In Tibetan Buddhism, the jewel and the lotus point not only to the deity Avalokiteshvara, but these two symbols also represent the two most important qualities of the mind that are needed to transform the ordinary person into a Buddha or enlightened being," he said. "The lotus represents wisdom and the jewel represents compassion. As a lotus is born in a muddy pond, but blossoms fully above the pond; it is unstained by the fault of the mud, it is pristine and pure. Similarly the wisdom that grows in the lives and hearts of ordinary beings like us is also unstained by the faults of our confusion and other destructive emotions. Just as a jewel like a diamond, is valuable—and can remove the pain and suffering of poverty—the compassionate heart helps eliminate the suffering of oneself and others. This is beautifully captured in His Holiness the Dalai Lama's often spoken statement, 'If you want to be happy, practice compassion. If you want others to be happy, practice compassion. From this perspective, the meaning of Om Mani Padme Hum can be understood as, 'May the Jewel and the Lotus Holder (i.e. Avalokiteshvara) inspire me to cultivate a union of wisdom and compassion, so that I can transform my body, speech and mind into enlightened body, speech and mind.'"

This is why the lotus and the jewel are two of the most commonly used symbols for a human being in Eastern philosophy.

I'd like to share another interpretation I've learned about the lotus. As any gardener knows, flowers and plants are not guaranteed to grow simply because you plant a seed. They have to be nurtured, watered, fed, and cared for. The lotus, too, will only bloom if there are proper conditions.

It symbolizes that humans of the earth are surrounded by temptation to do immoral things as well as being vulnerable to people who might wish to harm us. In essence, there is no scarcity of mud, and humans can easily become stuck in the mud of life. But like the lotus, and despite the mud we are embedded in, we have the capacity to rise above it all and flower. Humans can arise from the darkest places and find a way to thrive.

## Another Way to See the Jewel

It is believed by many Buddhists that we have that ability to lift up out of the mud, like the lotus, because of our Buddha nature. Our Buddha nature means we all have goodness within us.

In this way of interpreting things, Buddha nature *is* the jewel. And the jewel in the lotus is a metaphor for the idea that humans live in a place with a lot of mud, but have the ability to rise above it and flower, because they have the shining jewel of goodness at their center.

The lotus flower is also seen as a symbol of fortune in Buddhism. The rising from the murk and blooming above water also represents reaching a more enlightened state.

This is why Om Mani Padme Hum is the mantra that carries the highest representations of compassion and importance. This is also considered to be the mantra of the Dalai Lama—not because he is so special, but because the phrase serves to remind all who utter it that we are all equal in our potential to be good.

The symbolic meaning of the lotus and the jewel is preliminary to our next chapter on Tonglen, one of the most life-changing exercises in Buddhism.

# CHAPTER 10

# Tonglen — The Ultimate Exercise

*"With Tonglen, the goal is to change our attitude towards pain and to open up the heart so that we can be more loving and kind as we dissolve the pain around us."*
*— Dhaval Patel.*

TIBETANS HAVE AN ALMOST ENDLESS number of meditations. In addition to the great practice of the Four Virtues of the Heart, I love the meditation practice known as Tonglen. It literally means "giving and taking." It sometimes is called "taking and sending." It guides us in the compassionate action of taking away the pain and sickness of others and then exchanging it with the health, joy, and happiness that is ours. For this reason, it is often offered to those who are ill, dying, and even those who have died.

It may seem strange and frightening, at first. Yikes. If you are feeling good and healthy, why risk taking on someone else's problems? From the Buddhist perspective, you are not *physically* taking on their problems. You are symbolically using your health, strength, and consciousness to try to relieve some of their pain.

Think for a moment about a loved one who may be ill or hurt. Maybe it's a parent, spouse, or your child, or someone else you care about. Wouldn't you wish to take away what ails them and do anything you could to make an effort to heal them? It is not uncommon for mothers to wish it were they instead of their children who are sick or hurt. The idea of taking on the suffering of others is not completely alien.

When you stop and think about it, sacrificing for others is part of our culture too. Just think of our armed forces. Ask anyone in the military and they will all tell you that it is *not only* the ideals of freedom, or democracy, or country that make them brave in battle. It is also their allegiance and connection to their comrades in arms. They're not only risking or giving their lives for an ideal, but also for the person next to them to whom they also have a responsibility.

In a world that tends to be self-centered, those who sacrifice are heroes. We can all do our part to help those in need, but some of us will do it from the safety of our meditation chairs in our living rooms.

Pema Chodron, a Buddhist nun and author, says that Tonglen may seem to defy the logic of a world that prefers to avoid suffering and seek pleasure. Yet participating in Tonglen has many positive aspects. "In tonglen practice," she wrote in *Lion's Roar Magazine*, "we visualize taking in the pain of others with every in-breath and sending out whatever will benefit them on the out-breath. In the process, we become liberated from age-old patterns of selfishness. We begin to feel love for both ourselves and others; we begin to take care of ourselves and others."

Tonglen is not about your becoming sick from helping others. As with any practice, if you are very sensitive or empathic, you must protect and ground yourself beforehand. If you have a desire to remove the pain or sufferings of another in a way that does not require you to sacrifice yourself, Tonglen is a great meditation. It can be used in a large number of different applications, but it also ties together the essence of the Four Virtues of the Heart, as well as many other philosophical ideas.

## How to Apply Symbolism to Tonglen

Think back to what we discussed in the prior chapter about the Jewel in the Lotus. The Tibetan symbolism of the jewel and the lotus plays an important role in this exercise. Here's how we will envision Tonglen in this practice.

- **FLOWER.** The central feature of Tonglen is to literally picture a flower in the center of your heart, with a jewel sitting in it. Easterners are very familiar with lotus flowers; Westerners may only know of them from local botanical gardens. As we discussed, the lotus is strong because it is born out of the mud and blossoms into a beautiful flower above water. But if it is not familiar enough, you can instead visualize any flower. For practical purposes, let's use a rose.

- **JEWEL.** Then there's the jewel. Any kind of jewel is permissible, but again, because I am most familiar with the yellow hat sect of Buddhism, we will use the diamond, as is their tradition. A diamond has some very special qualities. It is the hardest substance on earth. Absolutely nothing can cut or even scratch a diamond, except another diamond. Diamonds are considered to be indestructible. So using a diamond as the jewel in your lotus means that nothing that you take in can harm you—the diamond will receive them and vaporize them instantly with no harm to you.

- **HEART.** And where exactly do we picture this diamond in the rose? We will follow what every practitioner of Tonglen does—we will picture it in the center of the heart!

- **BREATH.** Tonglen is always coordinated with your breath: you breathe in while *taking*, and you breathe out while *sending*.

Here are three variations of the many ways Tonglen can be done.

## Meditation: The Practice of Tonglen

The Tonglen setup will be used in all three variations. Remember to be mindful of the present moment. Stay alert and recognize any thoughts that arise in the mind. As thoughts arise, release any that get in the way of your concentration.

### Tonglen Set Up

Seated in a comfortable way, take the time to settle and relax yourself. If you wish, you can do a short body scan or use an anchoring technique, such as placing your hands on your lap with palms facing upward. Or, you might choose to take a few slow breaths to settle down and calm yourself.

Close your eyes and bring your mind to the spot between your eyebrows (sometimes referred to as your third eye). Imagine a tiny spot light there that can be moved around. Imagine it moving up about an inch. Then go an inch higher to the top of your head. Then bring that spot down to the center of your heart.

Picture the diamond in the rose in the center of your heart. Make it as real as possible by using more sensory inputs. Try to smell the fragrance of the rose. See its color. Gaze upon the sparkling diamond.

### First Variation of Tonglen

All variations of this exercise will be paired with one or more virtues of the heart. For this first example, we will imagine using it for the practice of compassion.

Bring to mind the person you intend to direct this to. Imagine them sitting in a comfortable chair and that you are seated right across from them. Like you, this person has a diamond and flower in the center of their heart. Imagine that a beam connects your hearts together.

As you look into their heart you see a small black spot the size of a coin (maybe a quarter). That pool of darkness in their heart represents all that pains them. It is the result of all their problems.

Decide that you will take that problem away. Concentrate on your breathing. Each time you breathe in you will take in some of this cloud of darkness.

See the dark cloud move up that person's throat and out of their nostrils as if they are exhaling smoke from their nose. Let the smoke collect in front of *your* nose. After a few breaths, take one big inhale and bring it into your heart. See the glittering diamond in the rose. It has the power to destroy anything that touches it. Thus, you are not taking any of the darkness into your body and nothing can harm you. You are safe.

Bring that darkness onto your diamond, and the moment the edge of the dark cloud touches the diamond, envision a flash which destroys it. All that remains is the sparkling diamond. That spark also creates a golden light that permeates your body. All the darkness is gone. Sit quietly for a moment and breathe normally.

Now that you have taken away the darkness, you want to send light. Again, picture the diamond in the rose and smell the scent of the rose. When ready, breathe out and with that outbreath send them the scent of the rose. Feel it travel out of your nose and across the beam connecting the two of you and envision it going straight into their heart. See the rose and the diamond in *their* heart and picture it glistening. With each outbreath send everything positive you have: Love, kindness, happiness, joy, and healing. Watch their diamond glow more and more, creating a bridge of golden light between your hearts. The two of you will merge as one.

This is the essence of the exercise, and you can use it to send one or more—or all—of the virtues of the heart. You can also direct it to one person or to different categories of persons, in the same way we discussed in The Virtues of the Heart chapters—yourself, a loved one, a neutral person, a difficult person, and all beings.

## Second Variation of Tonglen

This version is used to strengthen your own virtue and remove obstacles. Begin with the Tonglen setup presented above, and then continue with this meditation.

Picture the jewel in the rose in your own heart. Focus on the jewel as a symbol of your own pristine self, not affected by the afflictions your mind brings to your life. Visualize it turning into a white circle, which contains an unlimited source of love, compassion, and goodness. This is what Buddhist doctrine would call your pristine awareness, and it is imbued with tremendous healing power.

Now think about any difficulties you may have in your life, anything that bothers you or causes you any kind of distress. Picture it all summed up as a dark circle.

Offer a wish to yourself, such as: "May I be free from suffering and all of its causes." Then direct the dark spot to the jewel where it is instantly vaporized. Allow goodness and golden light to permeate your body.

Picture yourself happy and flourishing emotionally and say something like: "May I find happiness and its causes."

This version is not meant to be about ego. It is about making yourself the best person you can be so that you have more to offer to others.

## Third Variation of Tonglen

This variation is used to connect to another person. Do the Tonglen setup and then continue.

This variation came to me from two of my closest friends. They are a couple who have been together for 43 years now and have a really strong relationship. They spend a lot of time together, but they make their living in different ways. She teaches at a university and has the summer off. He does book-keeping and payroll services, so he can't take off for an unlimited time. Once when I was going away for an extended period of time, I asked her to house-sit and take care of my five pets while I was gone. It meant that she and her mate would be apart for several weeks, something that had actually never happened to them.

Of course, they could talk on the phone each day or e-mail each other, which they did, but according to both of them, the best way to keep connected was by doing Tonglen.

Each day at a specifically synchronized time, they went into a Tonglen meditation. Each of them would picture the other. Then they would connect their hearts. Each of them would look for any gray spot in the heart of the other, representing anything that was bothering either of them, or anything about how they might miss each other. Then each of them (simultaneously) would take away the darkness and send light and love to one another.

I thought this was a very interesting variation on the exercise, and it certainly worked well for the two of them. They always felt connected!

Try out each version of Tonglen and see how you feel!

# CHAPTER 11

# The Buddhist Approach to Happiness

*"The essence of philosophy is that a man should so live that his happiness shall depend as little as possible on external things."*
— *Epictetus*

*"The search for happiness is one of the chief sources of unhappiness."*
— *Eric Hoffer*

HAPPINESS IN BUDDHISM IS DEFINED as inner peace and learned wisdom, which differs from our Western view of happiness as pleasure. True happiness can only be attained by thinking outside of your immediate, external, physical needs and desires.

This is why cultivating the virtues of the heart is so important. You have to *work* to strengthen them, but practicing them is designed to ensure lasting happiness.

As my friend Dr. Jay Kumar, author of *Science of a Happy Brain*, says: "Happiness is not a promise. It is a practice."

Buddhism has developed many specific exercises to cultivate inner happiness through hands-on practice and study. It may seem too simple or offbeat at first, but it shines a light on basic human nature and ways in which we can improve ourselves and redefine authentic happiness.

When it comes to happiness, ask yourself these questions:

- Am I happy right now?
- What makes me happy?

Buddhism implores us to consider how our reliance on external factors can get in the way of happiness. For example, many people feel that they are unhappy right now but that they can and will be happy when they:

- Have enough money
- Find true love
- Lose weight
- Achieve physical beauty
- Are celebrated for being extremely talented
- Start a new high-profile job
- Reach the top ranks of their field
- Find a cure for cancer or some other disease
- Climb to the pinnacle of their success
- Become famous
- Have a bestselling book

The list goes on and on.

There is no denying that this culture compels us to look fabulous, dress well, make more money, and have highly successful work. We are influenced by celebrity couples and movies to seek a handsome or beautiful partner by our side. We are told from time to time when we are small that we must seek beauty and intellectual perfection in order to be accepted and celebrated. We are encouraged to reach for the stars and become successful.

But will any of those things promise lasting happiness and happily ever after?

No.

It's been proven time and again that these external goals do not bring lasting happiness.

External success and beauty, or even being perceived as having external success and beauty, may bring moments of joy.

But dependence on the external measures can create havoc and damage our self-esteem. In fact, Buddhism tells us that this outer dependence is part of the death knell for happiness.

Many of us know, through our own experiences of life's gains and losses: These outer manifestations do not truly make us happy forever. Yet we still strive for them as if they *will* make us happy. And we attempt again and again to feel better through achievement rather than through awareness.

## Happiness Is an Inside Job

Following our dreams for success, without inner strength and awareness, does not guarantee happiness. We fall in love with people, places, opportunities, and experiences and have peaks and moments of joy. But the material world cannot be counted on forever.

For example, the idea of money equaling happiness has been studied extensively, and most research says money in itself does not equal happiness. It's how we use it and what it may allow us to do that might make us "feel" happy, but money alone is not a cause for happiness.

One study entitled "Money Giveth, Money Taketh Away: The Dual Effect of Wealth on Happiness" found that money could "impair people's ability to savor everyday positive emotions and experiences." Wealthier individuals self-reported lower ability to enhance and prolong the positive emotional experiences in life. It suggested that having access to the best things in life may actually undercut people's ability to reap enjoyment from life's small pleasures.

This is not to say that you should not seek success, achieve great things, and enjoy the financial rewards. But we have to be mindful about what success does and doesn't do. And we must find ways to cultivate internal wealth and richness. In order to build lasting happiness, we must prepare for the notion that nothing lasts forever.

This is why Eastern spiritual traditions have always held that happiness is not found in external things, but in something that is inside of you *right now*. The Four Virtues of the Heart are designed to cultivate the ability to identify and connect with your inner world. It allows you to see the place within you that knows it can be happy without the need for beauty, money, or any of the external things. It is something that is available to all.

## Buddha Nature = Happiness

Buddhist philosophy teaches that achieving happiness is a natural product of something that lives within. It's known as Buddha nature.

The phrase Buddha nature here does not mean we will become Buddha-like. It also does not insist we follow the same path as the Buddha.

Buddha means enlightened. The person known as Gautama Siddhartha became enlightened and was henceforth called the Buddha, the enlightened one. So when we say that you have a Buddha nature, we mean that the seed or potential for enlightenment is already in you. Thus, happiness is your birthright. You don't get it from religion. You don't get it from a teacher; it is already within. Here's the catch: After years of trying to adapt to the world around you and trying to keep up with the demands of society, access to happiness has become obscured. It must be unearthed in order for you to be happy.

The Four Virtues of the Heart and other Buddhist exercises and meditations are meant to remove the obstacles that obscure or prevent our Buddha nature from fully blossoming.

Gautama Siddhartha was not only a great philosopher, but I would argue that he was the world's first great psychologist, thousands of years before the word "psychology" entered the lexicon. He understood the mind and realized that many of the problems we have are created or augmented by the mind. His philosophy teaches us to "look" at the contents of our minds and see that so many of our problems are caused by the way that we think. This is especially true for all our thoughts about happiness.

## Do You Know What Makes You Happy?

Many of us grew up believing that happiness is something to be hunted down and sought after. We've twisted ourselves into pretzels trying to keep up with the Joneses (or the Kardashians). Sometimes we grab onto certain philosophies because we have yet to formulate our own, or we blindly follow the lead of others because they seem to have made a success of their lives. Sometimes we grow up as an amalgamation of other people's wishes and desires for us—or their manipulations and demands. Sometimes we latch on to physical attributes and material success because we were taught it is the only path to happiness.

As a result, many people don't even know what does, would, or could make them happy. Many people who are seeking happiness don't know what happiness is, and this creates many problems for them.

Buddhist exercises offer ways for us to figure out our true heart's desire.

## What Happiness Is Not

There is a big misconception about happiness. People imagine that it leads to an unending joyous state where nothing ever bothers them and where they will never:

- Be sad
- Shed a tear
- Need a shoulder to lean on
- Be without a smile

They may not even recognize happiness because they think it means they should be:

- Free from all worries forever
- Completely content all the time
- Spend their days only following their bliss
- Living a life that only brings good news

This has nothing to do with reality. Gautama Siddhartha was a supreme realist, and he recognized very early that the world is not like that. This earthly life is not meant to be an unending state of glee that is completely free of pain.

The Buddha taught that if you live long enough, everybody you know and love will die. You and all your children and friends will get sick many times. Misfortune will befall you in countless ways, and nothing can stop that. The world will suffer hardships and dangers that cannot be completely avoided.

So what good is having a philosophy that has nothing to do with a pain-free reality?

Life will always contain hardships, so the idea that you can do something to remove all hardships is what makes things worse. No matter how much money you have, you can't pay someone else to die for you or buy health for a loved one if there's no medical hope. No matter who loves you or what you accomplish, tomorrow you can walk outside to find a tornado heading your way, metaphorically and literally. Or maybe you will just find a flat tire or that your car has been towed. There is always something in this world that can go wrong.

There is almost no end to what could happen in the way of difficult and challenging things. So happiness is not about preventing bad things from happening. They will happen. Into each life a little rain must fall—and we all know we have no control over the weather. So if the world still brings dire events into our lives and lays burdens at our feet, how can that possibly be happiness? Because happiness is about living with both the good and the bad. Accepting this is the truth about the world we live in.

Both positive and negative emotions are linked with mental and physical well-being. We need both. We need to:

- Feel a full range of emotions without judgment that identifies them as good or bad
- Learn that emotions are fleeting and feelings come and go
- Realize that happiness is the stability within that allows us

the strength and grace to process everything through our Buddha nature, without attachment

Being happy and leading a rich life are about taking the good with the bad.

## Impermanence Is Real

Nothing lasts forever. As sad as we may feel, working on true happiness from within allows us to prepare in a healthier way for loss. And it gives us the strength to know when it is time to let go. Grief is real and has its place in our lives, but it is not meant to be an ongoing state of mind.

Buddhist doctrine continually reminds us that everything is changing all the time. Trees and flowers will die. People we love and pets we adore will leave. We'll change residences, jobs, and maybe even families over a life time. Places we love will disappear in earthquakes, tsunamis, hurricanes, and other natural disasters. Eventually, part of the earth will fall away. It is not only all living things that die. The universe changes all the time, and parts of it will not last. I have repeated this numerous times throughout the book because it takes a while to truly drive this point home!

It is natural to feel sad, and I don't mean to be alarmist. It's just that for everything there is a time and season, and things we know, love, and cherish will be no more. Someday it will be our time to let go and slip off this mortal coil. Hopefully, this will be a long time from now, but anyone who has lost someone to illness knows that human life is fragile and loss is unavoidable.

It is no use wanting things to last forever because that is impossible.

## Immortality, Impossibilities, and Happiness

Some people wish they could be immortal. I believe that's a philosophical mistake. There are so many problems with this idea:

- Suppose that science came up with a procedure to make you immortal. Let's pretend that we can wave a magic wand and make all humans immortal right now. How long do you think it would take before the earth is overwhelmed like a garden overrun with weeds that kill off all life? How can we feed everybody? Where will we all live?

- And how about if only you get to be immortal? In that case, you must realize that everyone you ever knew will die. You will have to witness it and feel sad about it, experiencing loss over and over again. And if you could ask for one wish and that wish was that you be immortal, what happens if you get sick and are in severe pain and must endure it forever?

- What if you were given the wish to be immortal, and in perfect health? That should solve the problem, right? Not so fast! So now you are perfectly healthy, and one day you are in the mountains and get buried under an avalanche. Now what? You never get sick or get into an accident, but you are stuck there for all eternity! And while you are in there, most of the earth gets destroyed either by nature or by a nuclear holocaust. Now there's no food and basically no life to enjoy, but you still get your wish to live forever.

- What if nothing bad happens to the earth, but the sun burns out. Then what? In time the entire universe will be gone—then where would you be? In the meantime, not only every person, but everything you have ever seen will be gone.

Fortunately, immortality is not an option in our nonfiction world. It would take away the basic process of life and death. The inevitable experiences of life and death (and taxes, of course) are the only things that are guaranteed in life. Virtually every choice we make ultimately traces back to these aspects of our existence on earth. Without these things it would be difficult to set goals and nurture values. They give us a framework and context for understanding life. And Buddhism gives us the context for finding happiness within the framework of real life.

It is important to learn how to discern what will really make you happy and to match that against the realities of your life. This is not to say you can't have dreams. Buddhist philosophy asks us to use them wisely.

## The Key to Happiness

The first rule for seeking true happiness is not to seek the impossible.

It may be possible to be rich, beautiful, and the world's greatest actor, and to be married to the most wonderful person in the world. But it is not possible for it to last forever. Even if your good life lasts for a long time, all of these things will perish eventually. As they say, "You can't take it with you."

Understanding that, as sad and scary as it may be, can be so liberating. And maybe it will allow you to appreciate what you have, when you have it. Perhaps it will lead you to express gratitude for every moment. And, as a Buddhist practice, perhaps you will learn to expand your happiness by sharing it with others—those whom you know and those you may not know.

## Compassion Can Lead to Happiness

There have been many studies on happiness, and so many of them point to expressing and generating compassion as a happy place for human beings.

- The Harvard Business School was able to show that people are happier when they spend money on others rather than on themselves. The results were published in *Science Magazine*.
- One study tested what caused people to feel the happiest. Subjects were given an app on their phone that gave them a series of alerts, and they were asked, at any moment, to rate their feelings as sad, happy, or neutral. They would input their activity into the app to relay what they were doing at the time they felt certain feelings. The data showed

that though happiness can be found to some degree when we receive money, gifts, or praise, what made people the happiest was when they were helping others.

The evidence is clear: The more we are able to shift our preoccupation from self to others, the happier we will be. We know scientifically that greater happiness comes from love and compassion and helping others.

The eighth-century Buddhist scholar Shantideva defines love as the wish to give others happiness, while compassion is the wish to help free others from suffering.

Shantideva said:
*Whatever joy there is in this world,*
*All comes from desiring others to be happy.*
*And whatever suffering there is in this world,*
*All comes from desiring only myself to be happy.*

And in more contemporary times, when the Dalai Lama says, "My religion is kindness," he is referring to the love and compassion that is the heart of Buddhist philosophy. He is quoted as saying, "There is something about the dynamics of self-absorption, or worrying about ourselves too much, that tends to magnify our suffering. Conversely, when we see it in relation to others' suffering, we begin to recognize that, relatively speaking, it is not all that unbearable. This enables us to maintain our peace of mind much more easily than if we concentrate on our problems to the exclusion of all else."

There is no way around impermanence. When you try to hold on and control the ways of the world, it causes unhappiness. When you want only permanent joy and try to sidestep the rest of life, you will get hurt. And if you resist the winds of change and the inevitability of loss, you will be seeking the impossible.

But happiness is possible. It is a state of being in which you truly can embrace your Buddha nature.

# CHAPTER 12

# The Value of Struggle

*"What does not kill me makes me stronger."*
— *Nietzsche*

THE BUDDHA BELIEVED HIS LIFE of privilege prevented him from experiencing struggle. So he first sought enlightenment by denying himself food, comforts, and pleasures, and exposing himself to harsh circumstances. But it turned out that neither extreme was helpful, so he sought the middle way. He learned many lessons along the path. And he realized that when people acknowledge that life will bring struggles, and attaining certain goals may present challenges, it can make their handling of difficult situations easier.

Buddhism does not recommend that people manufacture struggles, but it is important to recognize they are part of life. This doesn't mean that people relish the idea—unless it comes in the form of entertainment.

Think of a movie or book that you cherish and admire or some work of fiction that changed your life. Chances are the plot is based on a struggle and that it includes loss in some form. The first thing any writer or filmmaker must do is give a hero and/or heroine a goal that they cannot live without and set up a series of conflicts, internal and external, for the character to overcome. The path to achieving success is fraught with problems and nail-biting drama. And the reader or viewer will travel the path with the characters, feeling the pressure of every roadblock and experiencing the pain of every defeat and wounding. Then comes the sigh of relief when the heroine or hero gets past their problems to fulfill their destiny. Yay!

You probably loved that movie because you could cheer at the end. You might even feel like you have achieved something by living vicariously through the conflict your favorite characters confronted and conquered.

Isn't it interesting that we love conflict in fiction but disdain it in our lives?

In real life, we prefer the rosy story with the happy ending. We want to avoid the losses and wounds along the way. We may appreciate the conflict in fiction and love the thrill of the ride, so we give ourselves permission to feel things—fear, terror, sadness, as well as joy, elation, and celebration. We experience a cascade of conflicting and complementary emotions through great stories, but we may be repelled or confused by those same feelings in daily life.

Could it be that experiencing those ups and downs through fiction gives us a chance to experience a fuller life, subconsciously?

One of the things that Buddhist philosophy and other traditions teach us is that we contain all those emotions and more. We often feel more than one emotion at a time, and we are constantly experience conflicting emotions. Sometimes it is as simple as feeling happy, and yet crying tears of joy that also make you feel sad. Or it can be as intense as loving someone close to you but sometimes not liking them.

When we become aware of this, we can see that difficult emotions are in our lives to teach us. And they help us identify what we would like to have more of in our lives, namely more satisfying emotions. For example:

- It's difficult to know what true happiness is until you have experienced unhappiness.

- It's hard to know true beauty in life unless you have been exposed to the uglier side of life.
- It could be difficult to know true love unless you have experienced heartbreak.
- Sometimes we do not appreciate the true value of life until we've lost someone or something.

Our real emotions are not limited to one harmonious or inharmonious note. They are a symphony. And they are forever connected as opposite pairs, such as: sad and happy, anger and calmness, fear and courage, love and hate, trust and distrust, and more.

Understanding emotions and how they work helps us understand that conflict is a natural part of life.

## Struggle in Everyday Life

There is a secret hiding in plain sight within those pairs. The struggles we face are all meant to help us grow. Without struggle there is no natural process for improving our lives. In other words, just like our favorite fictional folks, we thrive on conflict and struggle.

Consider a goal you'd like to reach. Bring to mind something you feel destined to achieve or something that would improve your life. It could be any of countless possibilities, but here are some examples to work with:

- You want to lose 20 pounds
- You want to enter a body-building contest
- You want to run a marathon
- You want to be exceptionally healthy
- You want to be a famous singer
- You want to be the CEO of a large, prosperous corporation

What would you have to do to accomplish any of these goals?

To lose weight you would have to go on some kind of diet and endure some kind of exercise routine. To enter a body-building contest, you would have to spend hours a day in a gym lifting weights. To run a marathon, you would have to practice running until you build up the stamina to run for 26 miles. To be exceptionally healthy, you'd have to study health, diet, exercise, and a host of related issues and change your lifestyle so that you eliminate unhealthy things. To be a famous singer, you have to hone your craft over the course of many years.

I have heard many people described as an "overnight success." From my observation, some people soar into the spotlight, but most of those *instant* superstars were about 20 years in the making. But we don't always hear about the blood, sweat, and tears of building a brand, writing a book, or having a hit recording. Because of this we may get the idea that attaining a goal is meant to be seamless.

In actuality, the accomplishment of all these goals has a common denominator. They all require struggle and lots of it. Your biceps don't get bigger just because you'd like them to. If you pick up heavy weights and gradually attempt to lift more each time, you tear muscle tissue, and it grows back stronger. It is *struggle* that makes you stronger in any way you can conceive.

Research shows it takes thousands of hours to master anything. Psychologists refer to this as "deliberate practice" and say it is a principle that guides anyone with the goal of becoming a world-class expert in any field. According to *Business Insider*, it means, "Practicing in a way that pushes your skill set as much as possible." Some experts say reaching the pinnacle of expertise occurs within six to ten years. Even if a world-class expert is passionate about their work and has a strong mission in life, you can be sure they struggled along the way.

On the flip side of the quest for mastery, there is a requirement to acknowledge the places we may not be so masterful and look at how to do better. The struggle to achieve goals means we must take the good with the bad and make lifestyle choices. For example, if you want to lose weight, you may have to struggle to overcome your urge to eat cookies and ice cream seven times a week. At some point you may fail and have to start again. On a deeper level, you may have to commit yourself to dealing with a food addiction.

The other thing that these goals have in common is that struggle sometimes goes hand in hand with being honest. It may be a struggle to tell the truth to yourself. The truth may be that you don't really care about losing weight but your spouse or mother is pushing you. So you may not truly want to take on the struggles of self-denial. Or perhaps you are struggling because you have been dishonest and don't know how to get out of a corner you have backed yourself into.

## The Story of the Cookie Jar

Honesty and using your struggles to develop character make dealing with struggles much easier. I got to test this within my own family.

One day I went into the kitchen and noticed that the lid on my cookie jar was tilted as if someone had opened it. I keep some spare money in there, so it acts as a piggy bank and not a receptacle for cookies. On lifting the lid and looking inside, I could tell that some money was missing, although I couldn't assess the exact amount. I knew it had to be one of my two daughters or my son, but I had no way of knowing who. My only real hope was to get a confession, but it was hard to imagine that one of them would want to own up to the offense. At the very least, they would be worried that my opinion of them would be diminished, not to mention that they would fear the coming "mom lecture" and the ensuing reprimand.

I thought about it for some time. I realized it could not be my young son and that it must be one of my daughters. I finally brought the two of them into my kitchen. I said something to them along these lines: "I have done my best to raise you with certain values, such as honesty and integrity. Here's the thing about those kinds of virtues though. They are easy to maintain when the circumstances for maintaining them are also easy. If I were to ask if you had done your homework, and in fact you had, I wouldn't be surprised to hear you say, 'Yes.' I might not have seen you complete your homework, but I know you have no reason to lie. So it would be easy to do the right thing."

I explained to them that the only way I can find out if they have truly learned about honesty is to put them in a situation where it may be a struggle to be honest—and where it might be more comfortable to lie—and then see how they respond.

"We all make mistakes from time to time," I said. "We all do what we shouldn't have done. I am not nearly as interested in what you have done or even why you've done it. I am interested to find if you can be honest when it is exceptionally difficult to do so. Now then, who took the money from the cookie jar?"

To my everlasting joy, both girls raised their hand immediately. They owned up to the fact that they had broken something in the house and took the money to replace it before I discovered it. Trying to cover up the first incident became even trickier when they tried to replace it with the "borrowed" money. But facing the struggle of whether to tell the truth set them free from the burden, and it allowed me to practice the Fourth Virtue of the Heart, equanimity, and shower them with compassion so they had the safe space to tell the truth. I was so pleased they learned a lesson.

## A Lesson for You

How exactly does my cookie jar tale apply to you and your equanimity? It applies because confronting a problem created by others is often a source of great struggle. It's easy to wish well for those you love. It's easy for you to be compassionate when those you love are suffering. It's easy for you to be joyful when something joyful happens to those you love. But it's tough when people you love disappoint you. It is even more of a struggle when you have to deal with a problem created by someone you don't like or maybe do not even know.

Buddhist philosophy tells us that we cannot rely on the path of least resistance. We sometimes must struggle to deal with a problem with our children, family, and friends. And we must struggle to treat friend and foe alike.

Being able to fill yourself up with compassion and shower it upon others is something that will truly build your character and strengthen the virtues of the heart. It will help you embrace and accept struggle and conflict, rather than try to run from it.

## Getting Beyond Polarizing Struggles

We all have people who get under our skin. Take a moment to reflect on these folks. For example:

- Imagine that you have a neighbor who annoys you to no end. You don't like how they behave, what they believe, or anything about who they are. However, you don't want to rock the boat and complain or vent because they live in close proximity to you. Besides, it's not in your best interest to approach them and vent because it would only make them angry and they wouldn't change anyway. Things would only get worse. Or bring to mind a politician you severely dislike, or even hate. Think of all the ways you think he or she is wrong or inept. Other than your single vote there is not much you can actually do about them and you wonder if that even counts.

- Whether it is the politician or your neighbor, or anyone else, acknowledge that your ill feelings cause you to obsess about these people. Severe agitation about people often leads us to ruminate and think about them constantly. We tell others of our hatred. We post our complaints on social media. We may even secretly wish them ill. Every time you see them or hear anything about them, your ire is raised, along with your blood pressure!

- Think for a moment of the anger that rises within you when you contemplate bad things about this person or, worse, tell others about how horrible they are. It keeps reinforcing the negativity. In the 1980 book, *The Angry Christian,* author Bert Ghezzi mentioned that venom toward another is like "taking poison and hoping the *other person* will die." This famous quote was often repeated by Carrie Fisher and others. The bottom line is: Haters are going to hate, but this has no impact on the one you are obsessively focused on. It only hurts you!

The best thing you can do for yourself is to stop obsessing about those you don't like. If you can't do anything better, leave them out of your life, your thoughts, and your meditations. If, however, you want to make yourself stronger and cultivate the virtues of the heart, include these people in your meditations and send sincere wishes that they: *"Be free from the causes of unhappiness, suffering, unhealthiness, and the things that cause strife."*

You can visualize them in a helium balloon surrounded with loving, healing light. As they float upwards toward the sky, you wish them well as they leave your life.

## Making an Offering to All Beings

Clearly, bodhisattvas have an edge. We mortals struggle when it comes to treating everyone equally and deserving of our good wishes. We don't like this one, we are annoyed by that one, and, ugh, we can't stand the other one.

Bodhisattvas don't have anybody toward whom they feel badly, so they can entirely skip the step of offering virtue to difficult people. For them, there are no difficult people, no enemies. So they go straight to offering their blessings to all beings, which means that they don't even stop at offering blessings to humans but instead offer them to all beings.

For them, there is no struggle to send compassion to all humanity. This is something we can all strive for. When we decide this is one less thing we need to struggle with, we reach a powerful point in our cultivations of the virtues of the heart.

Over time, you will find that as each enemy or difficult person disappears from your list, your happiness will increase; your compassion will increase; your joy will increase; your life will be easier; and your mastery of offering virtue to others will also increase.

When we understand the value of our struggles, we can aim to use them consciously and constructively to help improve our own lives and the lives of others.

# CHAPTER 13

# Suffering and Loss

*"All I teach is suffering and the end of suffering."*
— *The Buddha*

W E HAVE ALL ENDURED SUFFERING and loss and
we continue to endure them today. The pain can cut
deeply and scar us. We may sometimes feel we will
never recover. It is part of the human condition to suffer. But
we don't all have the skills to reflect on and manage our pain,
suffering, and losses in life.

In Pali, the original language of the Buddha, suffering is
translated as Dukkha.

It means a sense of hollow discontent that leads us to feel
we are living in an unhappy life. It may not be about physical
ailments, although it could be. It is more likely a pain in the heart,
mind, and soul.

Even those who seem to have love, comfort, success, and joy
in life may find themselves lost in Dukkha. Sometimes they don't
understand why. Sometimes they are afraid to find out.

## Owning Our Suffering

When people hear the word "suffering" used in conjunction
with Buddhism, it may make them nervous. They may fear that

Buddhism will *expose* them to suffering. But as I've mentioned before, Buddhism's foremost aim is to *remove* all suffering from the world. And the only way to get there is to acknowledge the truth of our suffering and its causes. First, we have to learn how to see the world as it truly is, not just through the lens of our own pain and fear.

## Everyone Suffers: The Four Noble Truths

The Buddha discovered that suffering existed all over and impacted all humans in all ways. This led him to study the causes. He boiled them down to two chief factors—desire and ignorance.

You don't need Buddhism to tell you that you are in pain and despair. But Buddhism can offer glimmers of how to see through fresh eyes and cope in a healthy way. This starts with a reality check about the suffering in your own life.

The Four Noble Truths, discussed earlier in this section, are described as a Buddhist contingency plan for suffering. In *The Basics of Buddhism*, an article at PBS.org, they are elucidated in this way:

1. **The First Noble Truth.** Identify the presence of suffering.
2. **The Second Noble Truth.** Determine the cause of suffering.
3. **The Third Noble Truth.** Has a dual meaning of ending suffering here on earth, and in the spiritual life, by achieving Nirvana.
4. **The Fourth Noble Truth.** Offers a method for attaining the end of suffering and points to the Noble Eightfold Path (discussed in Chapter 6).

Through the lens of Buddhist philosophy, the causes of suffering might be explained in this way: Ignorance is lack of self-awareness and inability to see the world. Desire includes attachment or cravings for material goods, pleasures, fame, power, and wanting to live forever.

All these things can lead to suffering. But remember, the things outside of us are not themselves responsible for our happiness or unhappiness. It is how we perceive them.

## Think Back to the Snake

Do you remember the story I told you about the snake? One person was terrified when seeing a snake, one felt neutral, and one was elated about the snake. So the snake was not, by itself, responsible for what the people were feeling. It was a combination of a real snake *and* what the people thought about the snake— their preconceived notions.

Many things happen in our lives that can make us sad. If you are a mature adult, or live to a ripe old age, you can look back over your life and recognize that you have lost friends, lovers, jobs, relatives, money, and countless other things. The reality of impermanence will live longer than we do. Everything changes— constantly.

Our suffering is magnified greatly when we forget this truth.

## Everything Must Change

Of course, we will be sad when we lose someone or something, but that is greatly amplified by the fact that we often begin to think: *Why me? This shouldn't have happened? Death is so unfair.* It is intensified by the feeling that we just can't face the fact that it has happened. Often that means, that we are not simply sorry for our loss—we grieve it.

We may become obsessed with the loss and take on the burden of grief, which can disable us to the point of not being able to function. So when we talk about the causes of suffering, we don't mean the actual things that happened, but our reaction to them. Yes, death of a loved one is heartbreaking, but the loss is not supposed to sentence us to a lifetime of misery. Death is a part of life. If we cling to our losses and perceive them as punishments or wrongs, we suffer dearly. When we accept the impermanence of life, we suffer less.

Try to think this way: If somebody you love dies, of course you will feel sad about it. But if you can remember that this person had a fervent desire for you to be happy, then you would not want to spend the rest of your life lost to grief.

You owe it to your loved one, at some point, to heal your heart and go back to your life.

You can remember them forever. You can carry them with you forever. You can be even closer to them in death than you were in life. And you can focus on all the good things about them, about what they have taught you, and on the virtues in them that you admired. But it is also your responsibility, after an appropriate amount of time, to go back to life. It is lack of living that causes more suffering than the loss itself.

In the spirit of their love, you can do your best to learn from all they taught you. You can try to honor them and their lives by using what they gave you to help you thrive and to be happy once again. Resisting loss only causes pain.

## Compassion for Those Suffering

All of us will age and die, and get sick, and suffer losses. You have limited power to protect others (or yourself) from this. But it never hurts to offer kindness. Give to others that which you would hope to receive yourself in difficult times.

Compassion does *not* mean that you feel sorrow or pity. You can respond to others who are suffering with practical kindness, for example:

- Ask, "How can I help?"
- Listen to them if they need to talk
- Bear witness to their pain without making comments
- Give a hug or a gentle squeeze
- See if there is something they need, like groceries or running a few errands for them

When someone has suffered through a loss or misfortune, there are often physical things you can do to help them keep their lives running. Sometimes, if you are able, you can donate money, or purchase things they cannot afford that would make their lives easier. But the mere fact that you care is often a very big help to people who are going through a hard time. It's also very inspirational to stand with a person in hard times. By letting them know that *you* haven't given up on them, you're communicating that *they* should not give up on themselves.

If it is someone in your family, you can say to your loved one: "If it is important to you, then it is important to me. How can I help you?"

## Helping Others Helps You

In raising children, I always say there are no mistakes, just learning opportunities. Similarly, I try to adopt that philosophy in all things in life. There will always be issues in our lives. How we deal with these issues is the important thing. I believe we have a lot to learn from helping others through suffering. And if it doesn't feel right or you don't enjoy it, let it go. If you find value, do it over and over again.

As we constantly widen the circle of care for others, compassion helps to dissolve the boundaries between people.

Compassionate response to another person who is suffering is a beautiful exercise to cultivate the virtues of the heart in ourselves. Once we have mastered the art of opening our hearts in loving-kindness to ourselves, it will be easy to extend that to others.

# CHAPTER 14

# Buddhism and Self-Esteem

*"You, yourself, as much as anybody in the entire universe, deserve
your love and affection."*
— *The Buddha*

IN AMERICA, AND TO A lesser extent Europe, we are afflicted
by low self-esteem, self-contempt, and self-denigration.
To other cultures, such as Tibetans, this seems bizarre. The
Tibetan language does not even have a word for guilt.

The Dalai Lama was amazed to learn about self-contempt
and couldn't believe it at first. He checked with some Westerners,
and they confirmed this for him. He was quite perplexed and then
asked if, in spite of this, they still wanted to be happy.

He was told that, in spite of the fact that the people themselves
may not feel worthy of being happy, they still *wanted* to be happy.
Assured that people would like to be happy and free from strife,
he was relieved—because Buddhist philosophy is focused on the
concept that *all beings want to be happy* and under no condition
would they think it is wrong for people to want to be happy.

In fact, the desire to be happy is an inner striving that we
are born with. Our Buddha nature wants to realize itself, and this
is something to be embraced. The Buddha once taught that "A
person who loves himself will never harm another."

This is why, in the Four Virtues of the Heart, three of the four exercises start with making ourselves the first benefactor of our good wishes. Buddhists encourage self-love, and they do not see it as arrogant or self-centered. They believe it is an essential part of life.

## Letting Go of Comparisons

One of the things that destroys our self-esteem and balance is the way we compare ourselves to others.

Suppose you need a car and want to figure out which car is better than another. You would consider many factors and features, such as: How good is the gas mileage? What is the sticker price? What kind of the navigation system does it have? Does it have good safety features? Sometimes this works, but other times it doesn't. One car might be better on six things while the other car is better on six different things. Then you have to decide which factors have the most value to you. It's such a tough choice, but as a good consumer you try to figure out the best deal.

Humans tend to compare themselves to others as if judging the features of a car. It's like looking longingly at neighbor's new Ferrari and beating yourself up for driving your ten-year-old Corolla.

But individuals are infinitely more complex than automobiles, and you could find countless things to compare. If we compare a million human features, how can we possibly decide one is better than the other? There are far too many factors to consider. You can say someone is taller, older, younger, smarter, prettier, funnier, stronger, more talented, or more interesting. You can judge someone for their career, financial status, home, how they treat their children and spouse, and whether they seem like a kind person. But there is truly no way to put multiple humans in a car lot and compare their lives and qualities the way you can with cars.

There is no effective method for comparing people. Each person is unique, multi-faceted, and incomparable. And you are too, so there is no way to compare yourself to others in a way that is truly practical and scientific, let alone healthy.

And yet we compare ourselves to other people constantly and judge ourselves harshly when we feel we do not measure up.

Each person is better at some things and not great at other things. Some people are far worse at certain skills and excel in other ways. For example, you may be a great driver, a good cook, and an excellent accountant. You may have a friend who can't drive, cook, or keep track of finances, but he is a skilled nurse, can build bridges, or is a great writer. And those are just tiny aspects of who they are.

We can't compare one human to another. It's impossible. So why waste your time and why hurt yourself comparing who you are to someone else?

## We Are Not Perfect

The other key to Buddhist belief is that we are not perfect. The person you may compare yourself to is not perfect—even though you may imagine they are. By the same token, you are not perfect either. It is self-defeating and painful to hold yourself to the ideal of perfection.

I'm not saying it is easy to let go of the need to have things be perfect or to be a perfect person. But the stress will wear you down over time and can even cause you to freeze out of fear of not doing things flawlessly. It can cause you to self-harm or to berate yourself because you feel you are constantly missing the mark. Humans are meant to make mistakes. That's how we learn and grow. Even the Buddha made mistakes.

We all have imperfections. And there is always room to grow and improve. It is healthy to become aware of things we would like to improve, but it is not healthy to hold ourselves to unreal standards. Our imperfections are part of what makes us unique, one-of-a-kind beings. Instead of denying that we have any imperfections, let's accept them and know we are worthy as is. Once we accept them in a healthy way, we are in a position to make conscious changes.

I personally believe we are all unique and miraculous. Sometimes we need a little help in seeing that for ourselves. I recommend writing these words on a Post-it note and placing it on your mirror or computer, where you can see it and say many times a day: "I am worthy of respect and admiration, just as I am."

## Self-Love Comes First

The most important lesson you can learn is to be kind to yourself first.

You can't give away money unless you have some to give away. You can't take care of others if you don't take care of yourself too. And you can't send out much love to others if you don't have any for yourself. No one can pour from an empty cup, so the first cup to fill up with compassion is yours.

People who are overly critical of themselves apply the same rules to others. They tend to criticize everyone for everything under sun. They call other people names to their face or behind their back, and they find fault in everything that person does. You will see the same patterns of behavior in critical people. And you can be sure that if they call you an idiot for making a mistake, they do the same to themselves.

It's challenging to be around people who find fault with everything and everyone. And this is true for those who find fault with themselves all the time. The good thing is that becoming aware of the ways you insult yourself gives you a chance to cultivate love for yourself.

You might start by practicing on an insult or derogatory comment hurled at you by a critical person. Start getting in the habit of sending love and compassion to that person. If someone says, "You. Screwed. Up!" send a wave of love their way. And keep practicing. Eventually that love wave will take on the power of quantum physics, as you learn to counteract the wrath of another person toward you by sending love and compassion.

Then, you can practice on yourself. Every time you hear

yourself saying something negative or accusing to yourself, send yourself love and compassion. For example, have you ever dropped a vase of flowers that broke on the floor and then started cursing at yourself? I know I have, and I've punctuated the moment with a loud, "I am such an idiot."

If you find yourself in a situation where you are likely to berate yourself, send love and pour out compassion—to you. That is the moment of power in which you can love and accept yourself, despite the fact that you are not perfect and regardless of any way you may have messed up.

In the moment it occurs, resolve to cultivate love for yourself. Resolve to accept yourself with all your faults. It doesn't mean you love your faults and want to pat yourself on the back for mistakes. It means you are human. And only when you accept your humanness can you start to put in corrections to certain behaviors.

## Cultivating Self-love

My mom had a plaque on her wall for all of my life that made a great impact. It was a saying by Helen Steiner Rice, and it read: "Love works in ways that are wonderful and strange. There is nothing in life that love cannot change."

Love is by far the greatest medicine.

We've been focusing on the self, and this is a very important foundation. It is extremely important to learn to be kind and loving to yourself. Most of the ways you can learn to love and help others starts with learning to be kind to yourself and to love yourself. Loving-kindness to all beings is a key aspect of Buddhism. And in the Christian Bible there is a story where, essentially, Jesus is asked, "Which is the greatest or most important of the Commandments?" The Bible tells us that Jesus said: "Love thy neighbor as thyself." The implicit statement was that you should love yourself.

Do your best to send kindness to yourself at every opportunity. Practice will help you get to the point in life where you don't spend time in negative self-talk.

## Self-Compassion Leads to Self-Esteem

There is no doubt in my mind that the first stop on the road to self-esteem is self-compassion. It always starts with finding a deep love and acceptance for self. This is not always easy, at first. We tend to wear masks that hide our goodness—even from ourselves.

Many of us are struggling to find out who we are. Perhaps people have forgotten our interconnectedness with all beings. Perhaps the changing world we live in has altered us so much that we have to work even harder to find our personal truths and happiness. Some of us are suffering from lack of access to good role models and depletion of the soul from life's hardships. Some of us are taken advantage of by those who operate with a personal philosophy guided by self-absorption.

It's time to awaken from the illusion of separateness from the world and from the separateness from our true nature. This is why compassionate self-awareness is key.

You must be your first compassion project. So take a moment to acknowledge the starting point. Try to be honest and to refrain from self-judgment. There are no wrong answers.

- On a scale of one to ten, how much self-compassion do you have?
- During moments of self-talk, do you tend to say positive or negative things about yourself?
- Do you sometimes have a hard time believing you are worthy of good things in life?
- Do you often take care of others and not yourself?
- One a scale of one to ten, how compassionate are you toward others?

Buddhism offers meditations and language for self-love and compassion. The more you practice cultivating appreciation of yourself, the more your self-awareness will grow—and the more you will have to offer others.

# CHAPTER 15

# Buddhism and Science

*"Do not believe in anything simply because you have heard it. Do not believe in anything simply because it is spoken and rumored by many. Do not believe in anything simply because it is found written in your religious books. Do not believe in anything merely on the authority of your teachers and elders. Do not believe in traditions because they have been handed down for many generations. But after observation and analysis, when you find that anything agrees with reason and is conducive to the good and benefit of one and all, then accept it and live up to it."*
— *The Buddha, in the Kalama Sutta*

ONE OF THE THINGS I deeply appreciate about the Tibetan Buddhist tradition is its compatibility with science. A core sentiment about the Buddha's teachings is that they can be measured against Western science and cognitive behavioral science. The belief by many is that Buddhism is evidence-based, just as science is. This is a philosophy that truly urges people, when in doubt, to dive into a deeper inquiry and make a decision based on facts.

His Holiness the Dalai Lama has always insisted that people must question everything and accept truths based on evidence—even spiritual truths. In the time that I have spent with him and the monks in his order, I've grown very fond of his approach. A lot of it makes sense to me, so I'd like to share some of the wisdom and contributions he's made to our world via blending science and Buddhism.

He once told *Scientific American* this: "Suppose that something is definitely proven through scientific investigation that a certain hypothesis is verified or a certain fact emerges as a result of scientific investigation. And suppose, furthermore, that that fact is incompatible with Buddhist theory. There is no doubt that we must accept the result of the scientific research."

It's so rare to hear a leader of his stature speak in that way.

And there is such a great benefit to have the freedom to choose what, if anything, you want from a particular philosophy—as opposed to being pressured to accept all of it.

When cherished Buddhist beliefs and practices are interpreted through the lens of science, it helps people to:

- Step out of the idea that Buddhism must be experienced as a religion.
- Discover the practical terms in which Buddhism can help them understand themselves and their world.
- Look at things critically and not just "believe" because a spiritual leader told them to.

To my mind, this kind of liberation can make it so much easier to explore any new tradition without the pressure of having to "convert" or go "all in."

## Marrying Buddhism and Science

One of the reasons that science and Buddhism have become so interlinked in recent years is that the Dalai Lama has taken great steps toward building bridges between Western science and Buddhist science.

The results of his commitment have made a significant impact. He said in a 2018 visit to Japan that it is time to bring science into the human experience in a way that leads to greater emotional stability and happiness. "Scientists' brilliant minds have predominantly focused on the physical world," he told the audience. "But human beings are not just physical beings. We also have feelings and consciousness. It's appropriate that scientists learn about the inner world of mind and emotions."

He also stressed that the violence escalating in the world makes it essential to study the connection between science and emotions. Out-of-control emotions are a big part of the problem of violence. He described it as a "crisis of emotion" and said that individuals also have to play a role in their own healing. Emotions will not go away only through the act of prayer, he said, "but by training our mind. In order to train our mind, we should have full knowledge about the whole system of our emotions and mind."

One of the ways the Dalai Lama approached this scientifically was to work with scientist Paul Ekman on a process called "mind mapping." Buddhist practitioners would sustain key states of attention and awareness, and their reports of what they were experiencing gave reliable firsthand feedback. This helped with the development of a comprehensive chart of the human mind that can be applied to how various parts of the brain are impacted by emotion.

## Dalai Lama, Scientist

The 2019 documentary, "Dalai Lama, Scientist," shows the progress His Holiness has made in launching discussions and inquiries with world scientists, as well as the programs he's helped launch that are making a huge impact. It also explains the Tibetan leader's proclivity toward scientific inquiry.

The Dalai Lama has always been curious about how things work. From the earliest age, he was known to take apart clocks, movie projectors, and other devices in an attempt to learn how they function. As a child monk, young Tenzin Gyatso (his birth name) had a telescope in his palace in Lhasa that allowed him to explore the moon and show where "moonlight" truly came from. His inquisitive mind always wanted to know more. At that time, living and being educated in Tibet, he had no access to the study of science. However, his order, the Gelug or yellow hat order, has always stressed logic and reasoning, so he was no stranger to the basic principles and methods of science.

Unfortunately, the Chinese invasion of Tibet drove him out of his country, and he now lives in exile in Northern India. As the religious and political leader of Tibet, he was forced to flee and establish a home for himself and the exiled Tibetan people in India. He has done so successfully. His exile has turned out to be fortunate for the rest of the world, especially the Western world, because the philosophies and methods of Tibetan Buddhism have been made widely available to us, to our benefit.

Living in exile also brought him into contact with people he was unlikely to meet in Tibet, including many brilliant scientists. Being an especially curious person, he instituted numerous meetings with scientists from many fields, including physicists, biologists, and neuroscientists. He helped establish the Mind and Life Institute, an organization that gathers scholars and scientists from different disciplines; they look at how Western science explains the world and explore ways to incorporate contemplative practices into various fields of study.

In the decades since he escaped Tibet, he has initiated many thought-provoking dialogues with some of the most eminent scientists in the world. It led to both an exchange of ideas and a solidification of the similarities between Western and Buddhist science.

"I am a simple Buddhist monk, but at the same time, individually, I have become very close with scientists," says His Holiness, at the end of the "Dalai Lama, Scientist," documentary. "In our training, reason has become very important. So this scientific way, it compels us to think how to analyze data, findings. Translate into action new ideas, new way." He points out that some of the scientists were skeptical at first, but are genuinely interested in making this a better world.

He went on to say that there is great power in skepticism. "(They) remain a little bit skeptical. But then, skepticism brings doubt. Doubt brings investigation. With that stated, all my followers, monks, scholars should not accept my teaching out of faith or out of devotion, but rather thorough investigation and experiment."

He concluded by sharing that he considers himself "half monk and half scientist."

## Reaching Beyond Skepticism

His Holiness was awarded the Nobel Peace Prize in 1989. The announcement came while he was in a meeting with a group of scientists, and he chose to stay with them rather than disrupt the meeting and leave. It was just the beginning of the advancement of the Buddhism and science connection. He was later invited to speak at The Society for Neuroscience and the National Institutes of Health. And he won the prestigious Templeton Prize, which honors scientific and spiritual curiosity. Each step led him closer to bringing scientists together for serious discussions.

Not everyone is on board with the idea that Buddhist practice is quantifiable alongside Western science, but the Dalai Lama managed to cultivate relationships with people in the scientific community from all over the world. They helped him explore and compare five major topics under the heading of "The Nature of the Universe." They included:

1. Cosmology
2. Quantum Physics
3. Cognitive Science/Psychology and the Nature of the Mind
4. Neuroscience
5. Molecular Biology and Genetics

His Holiness sought to look at these topics very closely and to draw parallels, where possible, between the Western and Buddhist approach. I took notes on this while watching the documentary because the results were so striking.

For example, here's what was revealed about Quantum Physics:

- *In Western science*: The observation/experimentalists cannot be entirely detached from the nature of the quantum level. *From the Buddhist perspective*: Normal things have no identity independent of the ways of acquiring knowledge.

- *In Western science:* Electrons appear to have no size, but they act like a mass point. They acquire mass where they interact with some other particles. *From the Buddhist perspective*: The lack of own-being of things accounts for their interdependent causal efficiency.

- *In Western science:* Quantum superposition and entanglement are being used to create quantum computers in an entirely new method of computation. *And under Buddhist science in quantum physics*, normal things have no identity independent of the ways of acquiring knowledge.

It's fascinating to juxtapose these ideas side by side. And the mere concept of comparing science to Buddhism also requires inclusion of the internal experience.

The late scientist Francisco Varela became a dear friend of the Dalai Lama. Varela was a prominent researcher who joined His Holiness in building the earlier foundation for this inquiry. He was co-founder of the Mind and Life Institute, and he wrote about and discussed the topic extensively.

"The natural meeting ground between science and Buddhism is one of the most active research frontiers today," wrote Varela in 1999. His thoughts were republished in an article called *Buddhism and Modern Science* that was published in 2010 by Mind and Life Institute. "What is involved is learning how to put together the data from the inner examination of human experience with the empirical basis that modern cognitive and affective neuroscience can provide. Such first-person accounts are not a mere 'confirmation' of what science can find anyway. It is a necessary complement.

For instance, unless refined internal descriptions are taken into account in current experiments that use brain imaging to study the neural substrates of emotions or attention, the empirical data cannot be properly interpreted."

This is why meditation, and the experience of the person meditating, has come under the microscope of the scientific community in recent years. And it is why scholars have come forward to learn and teach about the Buddhism and Science connections.

## Creating New Possibilities

His Holiness stresses the important of science everywhere. "Although my own interest in science began as the curiosity of a restless young boy growing up in Tibet, gradually the colossal importance of science and technology for understanding the modern world dawned on me," he shared in a speech at the Society for Neuroscience in 2005. "Not only have I sought to grasp specific scientific ideas but have also attempted to explore the wider implications of the new advances in human knowledge and technological power brought about through science."

In his continuing commitment to stand alongside scientists as they tackle the toughest issues facing humanity, he has invited and supported the creation of science-based programs to help contribute to the change he wants to see, and others have been created with his blessing. These include a number of important programs through Emory University.

CENTER FOR CONTEMPLATIVE SCIENCE AND COMPASSION BASED ETHICS. My dear friend Dr. Negi is the director of this multi-dimensional initiative at Emory University. It was first established as the Emory-Tibet Partnership in 1998 to bring together the foremost contributions of the Western scholastic tradition and the Tibetan Buddhist sciences of mind and healing. His Holiness the Dalai Lama inaugurated this program, beginning a long academic collaboration between he and Emory University. This collaboration has led to the creation of the center's three signature initiatives. They include the Emory-Tibet Science Initiative (ETSI), Cognitively-Based Compassion Training (CBCT®), and Social, Emotional and Ethical Learning (SEE Learning™).

**EMORY-TIBET SCIENCE INITIATIVE (ETSI).** This is the foundational educational program created to implement a comprehensive and sustainable modern science curriculum specifically for Tibetan monks and nuns. As part of this program, six Tibetan monastics known as the Tenzin Gyatso Science Scholars, are brought to Emory for a two-year science education. As of this writing, thirty monastics have gone through this training. After graduating, they serve as indigenous monastic science teachers at their monasteries and nunneries in India. While in the United States, they share their heritage with people they meet. They are always greeted warmly and are a welcome presence on campus. They bring a lot of happiness wherever they go and are regarded as cross-cultural ambassadors. They have been given the nickname the "Science Monks and Nuns." This initiative has created a six-year curriculum in the philosophy of science, physics, biology, and neuroscience, especially designed for these monastics. They have produced bi-lingual textbooks for each of these four scientific disciplines. This curriculum is now fully implemented in major Tibetan nunneries and monasteries.

**COGNITIVELY-BASED COMPASSION TRAINING (CBCT®).** This is a secular compassion meditation program based on Tibetan contemplative methods, developed by Dr. Negi. It is a systematic method for gradually training the mind until compassion becomes a spontaneous response to suffering. A wide variety of research studies have been conducted utilizing the CBCT® protocol with diverse populations including children in foster care, veterans with PTSD, medical students, and breast cancer and suicide survivors. This program is taught all over the world.

**SOCIAL, EMOTIONAL AND ETHICAL LEARNING (SEE LEARNING™).** It is a K-12 education program that is the culmination of an academic collaboration between His Holiness the Dalai Lama and Emory that has spanned two decades. The program conveys a universal, non-sectarian, and science –based approach for bringing the ethical development of the whole child into education. It is an international program organized around three domains: The personal domain, which focuses on self-awareness and emotional intelligence; social domain which focuses on compassion and interpersonal skills; and the systemic domain which focuses on interdependence and ethical decision making. SEE Learning™ complements existing Social and Emotional Learning (SEL) programing with a number of innovative strategies to cultivate attention training, compassion for self and others, resiliency skills based on trauma-informed care, systems thinking, and ethical discernment. Because of these additional components, Dr. Daniel Goleman, one of the pioneers of the SEL movement, calls SEE Learning™, "SEL 2.0." It incorporates the best practices in education and scientific research. Through a developmentally appropriate curriculum, available in multiple languages, this program is being implemented in many parts of the world. I was blessed to attend the launch of the SEE Learning™ program in 2019 in New Delhi.

As you can see, Buddhism has been an important philosophy in my life. And connecting with the Dalai Lama and the monks has inspired me. But there are many different philosophies to be explored and considered, and we will look into those in the next section.

# PART THREE

# Adding New Philosophies to Life

# CHAPTER 16

# Expanding Your Wisdom Tool Kit

*"The unexamined life is not worth living"*
*— Socrates*

A LONG TIME AGO I GAVE myself permission to explore different ways of thinking. Time and again I have experienced great comfort in philosophies that support my heart and soul. I have had the opportunity to study systems of belief of all kinds, through formal trainings and by following my curiosity to learn more about those that called to me. I hope that sharing my journey will help you take important steps onto yours.

We are very fortunate to live in a time where countless sources of wisdom are widely available. In our global society, we have access to knowledge through formal education and informal teachings. We can get books, stream videos, or turn on the television to receive learning from a host of wise teachers—even if they lived thousands of years ago. We can access information on any computer or device.

I have been blessed to cross paths with many successful people: World leaders, top entertainers, brilliant doctors, and scientists, and a variety of fascinating individuals. But more importantly, I've been able to developed relationships with many wisdom teachers from different disciplines, faiths, and philosophies. It has been my great privilege to have formed associations with great spiritual leaders from the Western and Eastern worlds. One of my friends is a Taoist priest. I have meditated with many Buddhist teachers and on more than one occasion, I have met with the Dalai Lama. And by now you know how much I honor the Tibetan monks and the sacred rituals and meditations they have brought into my life. Each of these people has something important to teach.

In the coming pages of Part Three, I will share some of the things I've learned and have found valuable, in the hope that they will be useful to you. For me, each religion, philosophy, or school of wisdom contains some valuable teachings that we can apply to our lives to make them better. But I encourage you to assess what appeals to you and to embrace only those practices that will enhance your life. You can always do more research on any of these topics, as well as find new sources of wisdom, as you continue your journey to self-awareness.

I am obviously very fond of Eastern philosophy, so you will see it blended in throughout this book. I like to use many different aspects of Eastern philosophy to make certain points. Not every early culture developed a philosophical tradition of its own. The classical Indian philosophers and the Chinese philosophers were among the first to set forth their now iconic views. Ancient Greece was also in the forefront of philosophy, and many of those ideas were adapted by the more modern Western philosophers.

In the next chapters I will share ideas from East and West, as well as secular and scientific philosophies that can be applied to modern life. These include insights into:

- Taoist Philosophy
- Hindu and Indian Philosophy
- Greek Philosophy

## New Philosophies to Expand Your Wisdom Tool Kit

Clearly, I am partial to Buddhism. You've just read many chapters that have outlined why. But my appreciation and love of Buddhist traditions does not mean I must identify as a Buddhist or reject other ways of thinking. And it doesn't mean that appreciating Taoism, Hinduism, or Christianity is cheating on Buddhism. I recognize that I find myself drawn to traditions that share some of the same or complementary features; or that may be very different and yet may have a similar message or goal.

When you begin to learn more about new philosophies, you may find yourself attracted to more than one. It helps to "unpack" and assess some of the things that appeal to you most about your favorite particular school of thought. Remember, each philosophy is more than just words. They offer concepts, exercises, and experiences that help you expand your wisdom tool kit.

For example, here are some of the things that summarize what I appreciate about Buddhist philosophy:

- It existed long before the Buddhist religion.
- Even in the religious versions, none claims to have the sole possession of truth.
- There are no scriptures handed down by "God."
- There are no infallible doctrines.
- Tibetan Buddhists, especially the Gelug order, debate their doctrines daily; they don't proselytize or seek converts.
- The Dalai Lama, on countless occasions, has said that people should stay whatever religion they are, and that they can still find great usefulness in the philosophy of Buddhism.
- The man called the Buddha himself cautioned everyone not to simply have blind faith and to believe in anything he said, but to think for themselves and see if they find the doctrine truthful and helpful, and, especially, to make sure it does not cause harm to anyone.
- It has beautiful and powerful language that expresses things that are dear to my heart and align with my personal philosophy.

I have an appreciation list for all my favorite philosophies. Each of them, like Buddhism, has expanded my awareness in numerous ways and they *all* intersect in my daily life.

## Look for Teachers and Friends

Another way to expand your wisdom tool kit is to find a way to have experiences related to the philosophies you are drawn to.

- Start with a visit to a museum, in person or virtually.
- Research all aspects of your interests on the internet.
- Find books that give you greater understanding, starting with your local library.
- Seek social media groups that are focused on the topic you are exploring.
- Access classes on the great philosophies and traditions online; many colleges offer continuing education classes on these topics for a surprisingly low cost.
- Get out in the world and attend conferences or seminars that are filled with people who have something to teach.
- You can also find many different virtual events that bring wise people into your living room.
- Travel to the home country of your favorite philosophy if you are able, or watch videos and documentaries related to your interests.

You can also learn a lot from speaking with people who were born into, or are currently practicing, the traditions you are learning about. Any exposure to philosophies that interest you will expand your awareness and your opportunities to dive in deeper.

## Expanding Your Choices

Having met so many people who struck me as being "living models" of what certain philosophies stood for, I was called to learn about The Perennial Philosophy, and all the diverse beliefs explored therein.

At first, I thought I would find that all philosophies were the same. I discovered they are each quite different and yet share a common core component. Each of the world's traditions seeks to offer something sacred or of value to practitioners. The method of delivery—and the overarching approach—may be different but all paths lead to something similar.

Let's use food as an example. Some people enjoy great diversity in what they eat. They may like Italian food, Indian food, and Chinese food, and they can choose to eat a little of each every night. Or they can savor that slice of pizza one day, enjoy samosa the next, and have delicious egg drop soup the next. They might have a favorite food that they eat more than others, but that doesn't mean they haven't developed a palate for all foods they enjoy.

Like food from different cultures, philosophies may all be different, but flavorful and nourishing. Like good food, all streams of wisdom nourish us. We wouldn't want to limit our diet to only one thing, and this is true of our appreciation of different ways of thinking about life—especially since we may find one approach works for some occasions and another approach is more fitting for other times.

## The Essence of Philosophy

There are two more important things you should know about philosophy. First, the word itself comes from two root words: "Phil" and "Soph." Phil means love and Soph means wisdom. So philosophy means the love of wisdom.

Love of wisdom has been a driving part of my life from an early age. Part of the reason I have always been excited to meet people is because virtually everyone I have ever met has something to teach me or some wisdom to share. I have always loved learning from different wisdom traditions and finding ways to integrate them into my life and philosophy. Truth be told, even the most "ordinary" people are extraordinary to me. Everyone I meet offers valuable lessons. We are all wisdom teachers and can learn from each other.

Secondly, philosophy has as its main goal, not just the acquiring of wisdom, but the integrating and uniting of all this wisdom into one coherent philosophy. Again, this philosophy can be integrated into your current belief system.

So my basic approach to philosophy, spiritual traditions, and all forms of wisdom can be summed up this way:

- Find what they have that is different from what I already know.
- Find something valuable to me personally, and that will enhance and integrate the wisdom I may have already acquired.
- My goal is to practice integral philosophy, which means to integrate into my life whatever seems valuable to me and enhances and improves my life.
- I don't abandon what I used to believe in (unless it is proven to be wrong), I add to it by integrating other ideas into my current beliefs.

My personal approach may be helpful to you in your journey, but you may also find a better way to explore philosophical ideas.

## Philosophy and Science

As a fan of science *and* philosophy, I always look for ways to merge the two. One of the most satisfying aspects about the philosophies I am attracted to is that they don't require blind belief or faith, but logical and reasonable investigation. Ultimately, I believe science can also lead us to compassion. It has shown that we are all almost identical genetically. We may look very different, but internally we are related. To my mind, this makes us family.

This is why part of my life philosophy is embracing traditions that show us how we can all peacefully live together and how we can unite this global world in a way that is mutually beneficial to us all. And this is the inspiration for seeking out philosophies that celebrate love, kindness, empathy, and compassion. Eastern philosophy has been concerned with these topics for thousands of years, but Western philosophy has come to this idea rather recently.

Now we can marry ancient wisdom to modern life.

I hope to make some of these philosophical ideas easier to understand and to offer ways to apply them to your wisdom tool kit and your life. I believe that when we find a path that brings us happiness and clarity, it motivates us to then do our part to help make the world a better place.

# CHAPTER 17

# The Philosophies of Pluralism and Relativism

*"There's no beauty without difference and diversity. Love unconditionally."*
— *Rasheed Ogunlaru*

*"To make a difference, understand differences."*
— *Syed Sharukh*

I'D LIKE TO STRESS, AGAIN, that your passion for one philosophy does not mean you cannot also be interested in another philosophy. You can embrace philosophies from different regions, time periods, and points of view. By the same token, your religious background does not preclude you from participating in other forms of spirituality.

Interest in a spiritual tradition does not mean you are giving up your own religion or even that you are looking at a spiritual tradition from the viewpoint of worship and divinity. Exploring other points of view should never feel like a threat to your own current religious views. Nor should it be something that causes you conflict. I only suggest expanding your mind enough to see if you can get past the confines of any limiting worldview you may hold.

If you truly study the world's religions you will find many interesting core philosophies. And when you consider these traditions from a philosophical viewpoint, they become secular. Being able to step away from religiosity and put on secular glasses can help you learn new ideas, and then incorporate these ideas into your current belief system. Pluralism and Relativism offer interesting insights on these concepts.

## Understanding Pluralism

Pluralism is a metaphysical doctrine that declares there are many different modes of being in life that can constitute reality. It is considered a "doctrine of multiplicity." We see it manifested in everyday life. It is a system in which, "Two or more states, groups, principles, and sources of authority can coexist."

It is often discussed as an opposition to the philosophies of monism and dualism, which are respectively called "doctrine of unity" and "doctrine of duality."

Monism suggests there is one way to look at things and dualism says there may be two major ways to see the same thing, or that there are two separate aspects of the same thing, such as the mind and the body. But pluralism tells us there is room for many ways to look at something or to include different aspects that may be part of the whole.

Pluralism, to my mind, gives a good deal of flexibility to seekers who may want to include more than one spiritual, cultural, or philosophical tradition in their lives. It leaves room for varying points of views.

Take, for example, the idea of pluralism in religion. This may not apply to individual religions and their particular doctrines, but it does apply to the idea that the universe is filled with many ways to experience faith—not just one way. Our world has the ability to recognize more than one ultimate principle. Diverse minority groups in cities around the country maintain their independent cultural traditions and practices; even in Utah, a state known for Mormonism, there are Hindu temples, synagogues, and mosques.

## Understanding Relativism

A concept closely related to pluralism is relativism. It is defined as a doctrine that knowledge, truth, and morality exist in relation to culture, society, or historical context, and are not absolute. Relativism started with the philosophical idea that what we believe is influenced by our culture, our language, and our society and time in history.

This led to the idea that everybody is right when you can see things from their overall perspective. It is called relative truth in the Western philosophical world, and in this case relative truth means that truth is dependent on your point of view. Furthermore, it is conditioned by innumerable factors such as whether you are Christian or Buddhist, American or Asian, a man or a woman, a prosperous person or an impoverished person, and so on.

If all truths and all beliefs are equal and the same, which is what relativism implies, then there is no particular reason to follow your own religion; you may as well follow *any* religion, since by the doctrine of relativism, you would believe that they all speak the truth equally.

The effect would be to diminish *your* beliefs, since clearly what you believe must not be any better than anybody else's truth. Relativism makes it particularly easy to abandon your current beliefs. But not every idea is a good idea, and ideas change over time. Even the Bible talks about slavery, because at the time it was written, slavery was the norm in the world. Clearly, we don't condone slavery now!

This is where pluralism can take over from relativism to help us move forward with planetary and personal progress.

## A Deeper Look at Pluralism

Pluralism gives us permission to pursue ideas beyond the traditions of our birth. True pluralism is about interweaving and integrating ideas from various viewpoints, but it does not require you to stop being a Muslim, Christian, Jew, Buddhist, atheist or agnostic—or any faith you call your own.

Pluralism does not, however, state that all traditions are the same at their base, and that, therefore, you must accept anything and everything as equally valuable. Thank goodness for that! Because if all religious ideas—or beliefs in terrible things like slavery or terrorism—were deemed equally valid, then we would have to accept all those who believe their way is the only correct way. We'd have to go along with people who use pressure or force or manipulation to assert that:

- Their religion is the one and only truth, without exception.
- They have the right to put to the sword all those who don't believe in "the one true religion."
- They have the right to force others to convert to *their* religion, as some spiritual traditions have believed.

Pluralism has an exceptional openness to truth, but it is not primarily about what we all have in common. Pluralism begins with the idea that traditions are different and uses that as a starting point. The object of pluralism is not to level the playing field and make us all exactly the same.

Rather than trying to erase all the differences among us, it is really about discovering how different peoples, with different ideas, traditions, languages, and cultures can find ways to live together. It's about:

- Finding ways to connect with each other
- Discovering ways to talk to each other and create dialogues
- Learning about our differences
- Even arguing and disagreeing with each other, but with civility and courtesy
- Creating systems in which we can live together in harmony
- Having respect for the philosophies created and adhered to by others, despite our differences

If we considered pluralism as one of the philosophies to live by, it would add to peace and compassion in our world. A commitment to that way of being, along with a very open mind, will enable us to learn from the incredible variety of people and philosophical beliefs in our midst.

## Embracing differences

It may seem cliché, but embracing the differences in people is a key aspect of healing our world. Obviously, the rejection of people who are different has created much pain and suffering. It happens in everyday life, all over the world, in small and large ways. History has shown us time and again that cultural trauma travels through generations; just think of the tragedies that befell the African and African American people taken as slaves, Native Americans forced from their homelands, and Jews killed in the Holocaust. Think of all the ways people still suffer and discrimination continues. Pluralism gives us hope of expanding not just our understanding of this philosophy, but of putting it into action.

It may start small, perhaps by treating a waiter or delivery person from another culture with more respect and gratitude. It may mean refraining from ethnic jokes or sarcasm. It may mean becoming more aware of the subtle prejudices that are embedded in our current life philosophy and becoming compassionately aware of the microaggressions that people of color face daily. It may mean finding a way to release the racist remnants of a childhood from another era. And if you are truly committed to knowing yourself more deeply, you may begin to look at different ways you have participated or still partake in any form of aggression against or mistreatment of people of different races and cultural groups. These may not even be intentional, but if you pay attention you may find that you have looked negatively upon people in marginalized groups. Look at these things not with self-judgment, but with an aim to move toward a more open and accepting way of life. Remember, you have tools that allow you to send compassion to yourself and to all beings.

## Variety Makes Life Better

There are certain elements in our society who seek to foster a world that excludes those who are perceived of as outsiders or who are seen as different. A world that lacks diversity would be a horrible place. What if we all ate the same food, wore the same clothes, adhered to only one belief system, enjoyed only one form of music, and all had the same color hair? That would turn us into a dystopian society that rejects everyone's beliefs and personal philosophies and insists only on conformity.

Nobody really wants a one-note world that lacks depth, breadth, and possibilities for growth.

One of the greatest joys of life is the incredible variety that is present in all parts of this planet. There are millions upon millions of species of flora and fauna. There are thousands of breeds of dogs and cats. There are millions of careers to choose from and so many different kinds of jobs we can each do. The food choices are endless. There are so many things to choose from that it can get stressful! There are also many philosophies to consider in life. The fact that we have choices, and that we exercise the right to make choices, is part of our strength.

I think it is a great loss to those who limit themselves from learning new things. And it is sad to think that they may cut themselves off from people who are new to them, due to fear.

America became one of the greatest countries and a world power because we were the "melting pot," gaining citizens from all over the world. People immigrated here with a myriad of skills, beliefs, traditions, and ideas. They brought new cultures and traditions, foods and music, and so much more. We can't all believe the same things. We may not have the same kind of work or education. Everyone has their own passion and goals in life. Our differences and diverse paths are our crowning glory. That's why I have no desire to tell you what philosophy to follow or what to believe! I would never expect you to accept everything I say.

## Everyone Must Choose their Own Path

It is also important to recognize that *you* cannot tell another what to believe. It is not that anything is stopping you from trying to get someone to see your point of view. It's just that it never works. If you have kids, you will know what I am talking about immediately. But beyond that, we cannot take our personal beliefs, religions, cultural mores, and/or philosophies and foist them upon others. We can't expect others to agree with everything we believe.

There is a very simple reason for this: Telling somebody what to believe will not make them believe it. I've been on this planet for decades. I can't think of any occasion when I was discussing politics or religion with someone, and they said: "Wow, you're right. I'm going to change my religion and my political party immediately."

Our outlook on life and our philosophies are fully formed in our minds. We are used to these aspects of our psyches and personalities. We have been raised with whatever strong faith, or lack thereof, that is a driving force within. We may passionately share, and perhaps even try to proselytize, but we can't expect to change someone's mind. Ever.

It may be frustrating if you wish someone would change their point of view because it would be healthier for them. But the fact that we can't force them to see our way is one of the great benefits for human beings living in a democracy. Not everyone is fortunate to live in a free country, but if you do, and if that is what you are accustomed to, you would not like anyone to tell you how to think. Nor would you want to be forced to eat a prescribed diet, be allowed to only follow one belief system, or have no say in electing a leader.

I know I wouldn't want to live that way. That's why I would never want to tell you what you should believe. You should be free to make your own decisions. I also hope that you respect others enough to let them make their own decisions, as long as their decisions—and yours—are legal, safe, and do not endanger anyone else's health or well-being in any way.

## A Common Ground

Pluralism and relativism get us off to a good start in embracing diversity and cultivating acceptance of ourselves and others.

Although these philosophies show us we do not have to adhere to one correct way of viewing things, there are certain commonalities in some spiritual traditions that are worth noting because they can positively impact our world.

Many traditions take different paths yet seek to bring people to a truly transcendent experience. They may not arrive at the same destination, but they offer a kind of inner awakening. People are transformed by it; the change within leaves them with a new philosophy. Even though this experience is unique to each person, they may find that different philosophies or traditions may produce similar responses. For example:

- A sense of delight at being alive
- Seeing the world and life with eyes of wonder and astonishment
- Unconditional love for all beings
- A feeling of oneness with everything

Research has shown that ancient rituals, chants, and language can trigger this response in people while meditating, praying, or gathering in spiritual groups. From Hebrew chants, Hindu mantras and Buddhist sutras, there are certain experiences that evoke feelings of well-being, time and again. When people travel a path that leads them to greater awakening and embracing of others, they become less self-centered. They experience greater compassion. And their sense of self, their ego, has diminished.

These kinds of experiences can be replicated, so people may choose to do them repetitively through a consistent spiritual practice. You don't have to be a monk, a rabbi, or a Hindu priest.

And as I have said before, if you view spiritual traditions from their philosophical viewpoint, you can enjoy the fruits of these practices in a secular way.

## Do We Need Scientific Proof?

Some people will not venture into something new unless you can prove it to them in advance. There are studies and experiments that can connect spiritual pursuits, meditation, and other soulful experiences with changes in the brain and having a happier life. I have deep respect for science, but because of the limitations of science regarding these very subjective topics, philosophy is a more fitting vehicle. And it can lead you to trust in your own intuition.

Science can perhaps open doors to compassion, but it cannot offer a template for defining personal ethics and values. It cannot tell people how to treat one another nor does it mull over some of the bigger questions in life, such as: Why are we here? What are we supposed to do in this lifetime? For those questions, we must turn to philosophy, and in many cases, we look toward ancient Greek and Eastern philosophy.

# CHAPTER 18

# Greek Philosophy

*"History is Philosophy teaching by examples."*
*— Alexander the Great*

ALTHOUGH I WAS EXPOSED TO many people and cultures in my earlier years, my understanding of the universe truly opened up when I studied Greek history in college. I loved learning about the ancient beginnings of our world and the great myths, but delving into the Greek philosophers was especially mind-expanding. It showed me how to look at life from a different point of view.

I was fascinated by the Oracle of Delphi. It was especially exciting to discover that the oracle was a female—the high priestess of the Temple of Apollo at Delphi. The Greek writer Pausanias wrote that there were three maxims inscribed in the forecourt of the temple, the first of which read: "Know thyself." In early ancient Greek this was interpreted as "know thy measure."

The Greek philosopher Socrates is widely credited with those words and with the notions that humans must stand up for, and live according to, their nature.

Those words and interpretations continue to carry a great power. They set forth the idea, thousands of years ago, that there is a great value in self-awareness. This means that it was encouraged in daily life. It was a foundation for living. Many philosophies suggest that once we have self-awareness, we can focus on neighbors, friends, and even "enemies."

The long-lasting nature of the Greek philosophers is a true inspiration. They sought to define the world, not through religion but through intellect and reason. Their names are still known by many and their insights have lasted millennia. It still astounds me how their words and thoughts have been woven into the fabric of history as well as modern society.

## Great Chain of Being

There is an aspect of ancient Greek philosophy that I find especially enduring. It focuses on our connection to one another in a powerful way. It's called the Great Chain of Being.

The concept of the Great Chain of Being started a very long time ago. Someone got the idea that all things somehow connected. It was first mentioned by ancient Greek philosophers, Plato, Aristotle, Plotinus, and Proclus. It later influenced Western thought. Derivative philosophies were also seen to emerge in the European Renaissance and the seventeenth and early eighteenth centuries.

The original purpose of the Great Chain of Being was to place all things in some kind of hierarchal order. The general idea is that the universe is made up of an infinite series of forms. Each form in the chain possesses the positive attributes of the previous form and adds at least one other. These forms might also be considered steps that are interconnected and that enhance each other.

The earliest Greek versions of the theory, for example, looked at the hierarchy of steps in this way:

- Inanimate matter of the earth, such as rocks, were at the bottom of the hierarchy because they only possess "existence."
- The next step up was plants, which not only exist but are also alive.
- The next step up was animals. They exist and are alive, and also move. In addition, they have an appetite.

In the middle ages, the doctrine of the Great Chain of Being was considered a chain of existence with God at the top. The main proponent of this application was the Italian philosopher and priest St. Thomas Aquinas. He was recognized as one of the greatest theologians of the medieval period.

The medieval Christian version was a hierarchical structure of all matter and life, but it included classifications of divine beings. The chain of order began with the highest being and progressed downward:

- God
- Archangels
- Angels (and multiple subdivisions)
- Humans
- Animals
- Plants
- Minerals

This same doctrine was used in countless applications. Sometimes it was just a subdivision of another philosophical approach.

It was used with royalty, to show a chain that began with the king or ruler and demonstrated the relationship of the people to their ruler. In politics, it was used to show the highest to lowest rank in different kinds of governments, with democracy on top and communism and dictatorship on the bottom. In science, it was used for diverse applications such as creating an order for animals, plants, minerals, and for things that are considered the barest type of existence.

The main thrust of the Great Chain of Being in all cases was to show that there was an order to the universe and everything that exists fits in somewhere in the chain. In all forms, it seems to share three general features: plenitude, continuity, and gradation. There is often an abundance of things to include, all things included in each grouping go together, and there is gradation that goes from top to bottom.

This doctrine continues into the present but has been modified and adapted countless times. Its most recent incarnation is the philosophical principle of holons.

## Holons vs. Hierarchy

There are many people who objected to the idea of a hierarchy. They felt that using the term "hierarchy" was judgmental. They resented having people ranked against animals. And many people did not relate or approve of the ways St. Thomas Aquinas applied the doctrine. They did not want to see a spiritual hierarchy that ranked ideas and entities, but made human beings seem less important.

This is why Arthur Koestler addressed it.

He was a Hungarian-born British author and journalist. He had joined the Communist Party of Germany but quit in 1938, repelled by Stalinism. He wrote the 1940 anti-totalitarian novel *Darkness at Noon* and used his international fame to espouse many political causes and tackle complex issues in his writings.

He looked at ways to adapt the Great Chain of Being in a more inclusive and less hierarchical way. Here are some of the steps he took:

- He made the observation that each step in the chain possesses the abilities or powers of the previous link and adds at least one other.
- He coined the word "holon."
- He stated the theory that a holon is something that is at once both whole in and of itself, and part of something else bigger, and that *all things* are holons: wholes and parts do not exist in themselves.

This fascinated me because it reminded me of the segment in the "Dalai Lama, Scientist" documentary (mentioned in Chapter 15) that looked at quantum physics through the eyes of both Western and Buddhist science: Western science states, "The observer/experimentalist cannot be entirely detached from nature at the quantum level," whereas Buddhist science states, "Known things have no identity independent of the ways of acquiring knowledge." Holons sounded so similar!

Koestler died in 1983, so he was not basing his work on those precise insights, but clearly he shared the belief that there was a way to look at this concept without using the objectionable word "hierarchy." To do away with that, he coined the term "holarchy." His concept of a holon was adapted in countless fields, and his language became commonly used in the educational, social, political, and scientific spheres.

## Examples of Holons

It's fun to put this philosophy to the test.

Let's take, for example, the letters of our alphabet. Any letter is whole all by itself. But if I showed you some individual letters on study cards—A, C, J, and M—you would know that each one is a letter of the alphabet and can stand alone as one letter.

But if we pull out a Scrabble board, we remember that we can combine letters to make words. Words are comprised of letters and thus contain them, but their combination gives them another level of meaning that letters don't have in and of themselves.

When we take this a step further, we know:

- Words can be combined into sentences.
- Sentences can be blended into paragraphs.
- Paragraphs can become a page in a manuscript.
- Pages can be turned into whole chapters.
- Chapters can be organized into books.

Each step contains the lower elements and adds an additional power that the lower step does not have. This process can be carried on over and over again. And it just gets bigger. For example, when a book is bought by a publisher who has many books to offer readers, it gains additional power and prominence.

As another example, take an electron, proton, and neutron.

Each is an entity in itself. Combining these three particles makes an atom. Atoms combined make molecules that are bonded. Depending on the kind of molecule, this may lead to the creation of tissues, organs, or humans.

Koestler was quick to point out that holarchy shows that each step adds some other power. This is not about making a judgment, since the lower steps are crucial to the existence and potency of the next step.

- If you don't have words, you can't have sentences.
- If you don't have letters, you can't have words.
- If you don't have particles, you can't have atoms.
- If you don't have atoms, you can't have molecules.
- If you don't have molecules, you can't have tissues.

In fact, if you destroy a so-called higher link in the holarchy, it harms nothing below. If you destroy anything lower, *all* the things above it will disappear.

If you take away letters and nothing above lives on, there can be no words and sentences, and no books to read. The letters are the bedrock of the book.

If you take away atomic particles, then nothing will exist. There will be no atoms.

The lower entries in the holarchy are not inferior. They are the source of the creation of all that comes next. They are needed to build toward the higher steps.

## Turtles All the Way Down

According to the theory of holons, this chain continues infinitely—*everything* is whole in itself and part of something bigger. This reminds me of an old joke. There are dozens of versions of this joke but I'd like to share one I read by American philosopher, Ken Wilber:

A king goes to a wise person and asks: "How is it that the earth does not fall down and seems suspended in space?"

The wise person replies: "The earth is resting on a lion."

The king says: "What, then, is the lion resting on?"

"The lion is resting on an elephant," says the wise person.

"On what is the elephant resting?" the king asks.

The wise person replies: "The elephant is resting on a turtle"

The king then says: "On what is the . . . "

The wise person interrupts the king in mid-sentence and says: "You can stop right there, your majesty. It's turtles all the way down."

The joke tries to explain that world is resting on the back of a large beast or animal, one standing upon the other. There is infinite regress to lower steps. Clearly, we are in trouble if the turtles (or any of the levels below) fall.

## Applying the Theory of Holons to You

You are a human being. As such, you exist in your own right. But you are also a part of something larger—a neighborhood, community, city, state, country, the world, and the universe.

You are an essential being. You, in your own right, are important. Even in the great chain you have something unique: The ability to be self-aware. As Greek philosopher Aristotle told us, this is the first step to *all* wisdom.

If you long to help others and make a difference in our world, you have to acquire all you want to share. It must live within you. To dispense wisdom, you must have wisdom. To share inspiration, you must be inspired.

Your self-awareness enables you to reach out and inspire others to have deeper self-awareness. Then they will touch others with *their* self-awareness. And those folks will share it with others. And eventually there will be a critical mass of self-awareness that helps us reshape the world with love and compassion.

I continue to hold out hope that this theory can be applied for the betterment of our world. And I truly believe that you, as an individual, can be the first level for many changes.

# CHAPTER 19

# Hindu Philosophy

*"Be like a lotus... It takes what is useful and does not let the dirt
and mud spoil its beauty."*
— *Dadi Janki*

I HAVE TRAVELED THE WORLD OVER and have visited India many times. It is a complicated country with many dichotomies, but it has produced profound and long-lasting schools of philosophy. Many of the great ancient teachings have seeped into the United States, and we have great benefits from this wonderful culture in our own communities.

Interestingly, my first hands-on experience with a philosophy that originated from that part of the world was in the United States, when I was invited to a meditation meeting hosted by the Brahma Kumaris. The name stands for "Daughters of Brahma"—who is the Hindu God of Creation—and it is the world's largest spiritual organization run by women. At the helm was Rajyogini Dadi Janki, a wise and wonderful woman who offered inspiration for everyday life. I was taken with her kindness and enjoyed being in her presence. This led me to interview her for my first book, *What Is Spirit?*

The main teaching of the Brahma Kumaris organization is Raja Yoga meditation. It appealed to me because it was accessible to people of all backgrounds. It could be practiced anytime or anywhere. There are no required rituals or mantras. The basic philosophy was that meditation was meant to spiritually empower people. It was seen as a state of being that helps us get to a different level of consciousness. On a personal level, I found the meditations very beautiful and soothing. And I appreciated that I always felt accepted. When you're raised in America, you may believe you are not welcome to philosophies that originate in other countries. And in some cases, you may not be. But if you find an organization that sings to you in some way, give it a try. We can learn from rich traditions that allow us to partake without having to change our core beliefs.

I fondly remember that my early days of meditation led to a long-term relationship with Dadi, having spent so much time with her in her meditation group in Miami and also at events in Washington, D.C. I also grew close to Sister Jenna, founder of the America Meditates program and The Meditation Museum. She remains a dear friend and continues to help the world through her offerings and her radio show.

Dadi Janki died in on March 27, 2020, at the age of 104, but leaves behind her teachings, many of which are profound in their kindness and simplicity. For example, she said: "Let me tell you the secret to living a long and happy life. Accept from your heart whatever comes in front of you. Remain content, and you will also remain happy. Remain happy, and you will also be content. Be happy constantly and distribute happiness. If I am happy with everyone, then everyone will be happy with me." She offered many gentle rules for living a good life.

I appreciate the way the Brahma Kumaris philosophy could be applied to modern life, including through technology. There is a "Virtuescope" on their website (www.brahmakumaris. org/discovery/virtuescope) which is essentially a color wheel with twenty-one qualities or virtues. You can click on a button to spin the wheel; it lands on one of the words, and then an upbeat description pops up. On my first try, I got the quality of contentment, which came with this message: "Just by writing a list of your achievements you realize that you have everything you need." The instruction is to hold the virtue and the associated color in your mind to see if you can improve the quality of your day.

Obviously, this is a simplified approach to applying ancient wisdom to modern life. The Brahma Kumaris have their own particular philosophy. But they are a segment of the larger macrocosm of Hinduism, which is a vital part of the ancient and classic system known as Indian philosophy.

## Divinity and Philosophy

Hinduism is such an old religion that it impossible to track all those who brought it into being. There were many philosophers, priests, sages, scribes, and others who have contributed over the past five thousand years or so. There have been diverse eras of religious movements, and much of the ancient history is told through mythology, in great epics such as the Mahabharata, and through holy scriptures, and sacred texts. These include the Vedas ("Books of Knowledge"), the Upanishads, and the Bhagavad Gita.

Unlike the Bible and the Koran, Hinduism does not have one central creation story. In fact, it has many different tales, related to different divine beings. Like all religions, its specific tenets, rituals, and practices began long ago. It has religious laws and ethics. But it has something our Judeo-Christian culture does not entirely relate to, gods *and* goddesses.

While there is one primary divine essence, there is a pantheon of divine females and males. Much like the Greek pantheon of divine beings and the Buddhist deities, these divine figures have various roles, powers, and relationships. Hindus also believe that the masculine must be supported by the feminine. Thus, the main deities are paired with consorts. Hinduism recognizes three principle gods:

- Brahma, known as the creator of the universe, and his consort, Sarasvati, the Goddess of Wisdom.
- Vishnu, known as preserver of the universe, and his consort,

Lakshmi, the Goddess of Wealth.

- Shiva, who is known as destroyer of the universe, and his consort, Parvati, the Goddess of Love, Beauty, Fertility and Marriage.

Hinduism also has a well-known Avatar known as Krishna. His partner is Radha. They are often seen as the pairing of humanity with divinity.

In India, many families follow their own particular gods. Some are devoted to one god. For example, the Shaivites are part of the branch that is devoted to Shiva as the Supreme Being. There are other groups that focus only on Devi worship, praying to the all-embracing Mother Goddess or an aspect of Mahadevi or Shakti, such as the Goddess Kali.

There are many rituals for worshiping deities as well as a plethora of prayers, songs, and devotional music. Priests in the temples, as well as devotees at home, may perform worship and chanting to honor these divine beings.

There are more than two million Hindus living in the United States, so you do not have to go to India to experience the vibrant and culturally rich practices. They are available through the local Hindu temples and communities. There is a lot to be learned by attending holiday events that embrace cultural celebrations, such as the spring festival known as Holi and the festival of lights in the fall called Diwali. Hinduism is filled with colorful practices and is one of the most expansive, long-lasting traditions on the planet.

## The Ancient Pillars

Hindu philosophy and Classical Indian philosophy are interrelated. But philosophies of the ancient Indian civilizations stand as pillars upon which all other philosophies were built. They are taught through very specific, multi-layered schools of knowledge. Classical Indian philosophers existed in different civilizations at varying time periods on the Indian subcontinent. They concerned themselves primarily with philosophical problems and exploring the bigger questions related to cosmology, metaphysics and epistemology, such as:

- Seeking understanding about the nature of the world
- Exploring and confirming the nature of reality
- Identifying ethics and the related religious philosophies

Classical Indian philosophy is divided into orthodox and heterodox systems. The orthodox schools include: Nyaya, Vaisheshika, Samkhya, Yoga, Mimamsa, and Vedanta. The heterodox (sometimes called unorthodox) schools included philosophies outside of the original standard Hindu beliefs: Jainism, Buddhism, Ajivika Ajñana, and Charvaka. It seems that the prominent differences between these two sides of the philosophical equation are that the orthodox schools accept the authority of Vedas and belief in God. Some of the heterodox schools rejected the Vedas and did not necessarily have the same view of divinity and the soul, or outright rejected any religious form.

## Indian Philosophers and Mystics

Unlike Greek philosophy, which is filled with many familiar philosophers, Indian philosophers of ancient times are not as well known in the West. They included names like Maitreyi, Alara Kalama, and Aksapada Gautama and can be traced back to the second century. Many are known via their mention in ancient Indian texts and holy books, but the philosophical ideals of classical ancient India were not always attributed to one particular person. Philosophies that developed later—such as Jainism, Buddhism, and Sikhism—were more likely to be related to a particular founder or sacred figure.

Some philosophers are a bit more recognized than other, often due to the nature of their work and exposure in the West. Many of us know the ancient India philosopher Vatsyayana; if not by name, we have likely heard the work he is most known for writing, *The Kama Sutra*. It is considered the world's most ancient text on human sexuality.

## Gurus and Wisdom Teachers

Some great spiritual thinkers are called philosophers. But India also embraces a system of diverse but interconnected Hindu teachings from teachers that are called gurus or yogis. These wise women and men of modern times have become more well-known than their predecessors, since many have brought their teachings to the United States and elsewhere. Followers consider them to be sages and philosophers.

Modern-day gurus often come from a long lineage of teachers. For example, Swami Satchidananda Saraswati (1914-2002) was the founder of Integral Yoga, which embraces all faiths. His organization is known for a beautiful work of art that features a lotus filled with symbols of the world's faiths and includes the spiritual slogan: "Truth Is One, Paths Are Many." He was the student of Sivananda Saraswati (1887-1963), a physician who became the founder of the Divine Life Society. His teacher was Vishwananda Saraswati, who hailed from a monastery that was established by Sri Adi Shankaracharya in the 8th century.

## The Philosophy of Ayurveda

Another philosophy that hails from Indian culture is Ayurveda, an ancient approach to medicine and healing that is widely practiced today. It means, "The Science of Life." I have always been drawn to its holistic yet scientific approach. It considers the whole person and seeks to balance the individual by creating balance between the mind, body, spirit and social well-being. It began as an oral tradition over five millennia ago and it appears in the Vedas.

Ayurveda philosophy holds that there are three basic types of functional principles that exist in all people and all things. These concepts represent certain energies and are described by their

Sanskrit words: Vata, pitta, and kapha. These qualities exist in all people, but they usually can be identified in order of prominence. It is believed that people become diseased because these elements are out of whack. There may be a lack, or excess, of vata, pitta, or kapha. This philosophy believes in helping people to get and stay in balance so as to avoid illness. It is believed a balanced body can ward off disease and experience greater health.

In this system of belief, allopathic medicine is important because it saves lives, but it is focused on treating symptoms and removing illness through surgery, and not true healing of the causes of disease. Practitioners or doctors of Ayurvedic medicine try to help clients to a more natural path of health care. It requires lifestyle changes. And if you have not grown up around this kind of healing, it may take some getting used to because it is a specific approach, with special foods, healing remedies, and specially developed massages. If this path calls to you, it is best to find an experienced practitioner to see if it's a fit.

## Our Fascination with Indian Culture

India can brag about many things, including the fact that it was the birthplace of so many brilliant people, innovative ideas, philosophies, and spiritual teachers. It has the most ancient continuous spiritual philosophies in existence. The earliest sacred scriptures of any kind on earth are the Vedas. They were compiled many millennia ago.

It is a land comprised of a vast number of different cultures that were eventually united into one country. Even today, there is no such thing as the "Indian" language. Hindi and Sanskrit are well-known, and they are included in the twenty-two languages officially recognized by the government. However, it's estimated that there may be one hundred or more different languages spoken in India. It is known for Hinduism, but there are so many other spiritual traditions. It is also home to Sikhs, Jains, Christians, Muslims, and Buddhists, among other faiths you probably have never heard of.

I often think of India as the first place to practice pluralism.

We are blessed to be able to travel there and revel in the culture and doubly blessed to see how the Indian culture has been integrated into the United States. It is a prime example of how we can appreciate, embrace, and integrate ideas from various sciences, philosophies, and disciplines.

## Like a Rainbow

So much inspiration for life has come from ancient India, modern India, and all Eastern philosophies. And so much wisdom from those philosophies has blended into our Western world. America's greatest strength is that we are a melting pot for people and families of diverse nationalities who come here to offer special skills and new cultural ideas.

This makes me think of a rainbow, a symbol I associate with my mother. Everything that we ever see comes to us by the benefit of light. Light per se is not exactly something we see directly. We see *things* because light illuminates those things. But we don't exactly see the light itself. If we were to describe it, we might think of it as not having a color.

But in 1671 Isaac Newton discovered that light is actually comprised of seven colors. By shining light through a prism, it splits into its seven different colors. Raindrops (or drops of water as mist) can also act like a prism, and that is what we see as a rainbow.

I should also mention that seven is a sacred number in some Indian and yogic traditions, including the belief that we all have seven chakras, which are energy centers in the body. They are all different colors, and when connected and when in balance, we are in harmony.

So it takes seven chakras to balance our bodies. It takes seven colors of light to make a rainbow to brighten the sky. And we live in a world of seven continents. This, to me, is symbolic of the fact that it takes people and ideas from all around the earth to make our earth what it is.

# CHAPTER 20

# Taoist Philosophy

*"The Tao is empty. When utilized, it is not filled up. So deep! It seems the source of all things."*
— *Tao Te Ching*

TAOISM (DAOISM) JOINS BUDDHISM AND Hinduism as one of the greatest innovations of the Axial Age. Lasting between 300 to 500 BCE, this was considered one of the greatest time periods for the establishment of meaningful philosophical thought. In addition to bringing forth great intellectual systems, it led to great religious and spiritual systems. They became the basis for understanding the world and living life. They shaped the subsequent human societies.

And these ancient systems continue to be beloved in modern life.

China was the birth place of Taoism, as well as of many philosophers who sought to teach about how to have a good, ethical life. Confucius was the first wise man to become a great philosopher who offered ethical teachings; Mozi was another. Their work culminated Confucianism and Mohism, ancient philosophies of logic, rational thought, ethics, and science.

Also coming out of that time period was Lao-Tzu (also known as Laozi or Lao-Tze). He is often credited with founding the philosophical system of Taoism; yet Tao expert Derek Lin suggests that Lao-Tzu's role was to put into words systems of belief that already existed when he authored the *Tao Te Ching* (also known as the *Daodejing)* over 2500 years ago. Lin is one of the modern authors who translated Lao-Tzu's writings. "One of the reasons Taoism has such durability is, paradoxically, because of its flexible and inclusive nature," writes Lin.

The ancient sages who practiced the Tao were essentially interfaith practitioners because Taoism embraces all religions. This is precisely why Taoism has always appealed to me so much. Like Buddhism, Taoism is an extremely open-minded philosophy that contains no dogma. Its teachings are gentle and inspiring. The Tao is like an observation that life flows in a certain way.

Taoism started as a philosophy and not as a religion: There are no gods, no heaven and hell, and no talk of sin. This kind of outlook is called classical Taoism. Various religious versions followed much later, but they are followed mostly by peoples in countries outside of China.

The central tenets of Taoism focus on universal, holistic, and peaceful principles. It emphasizes cultivating self-awareness through meditation and certain spiritual practices. It espouses concepts such as:

- Effortless action (Wu wei)
- Naturalness (Ziran)
- Non-being (Wu )
- Life energy (Ch'i), which is represented in the concept of yin and yang.

## The Importance of the Yin Yang Symbol

It's likely you have seen the classic Yin Yang on everything from t-shirts to Feng Shui books to the office door of an acupuncturist.

This symbol hails from Taoism, and it embodies aspects of the Tao.

- It is a concept of dualism.
- It shows how contrary forces, represented as black and white, can be interconnected and complementary.
- It indicates interdependence of both halves.
- It demonstrates that one gives rise to the other.
- It shows each color in equal balance and equal relevance.
- Both are needed to achieve wholeness.
- The dark swirl is the Yin. It is considered feminine in nature, as it represents the shadows, the depths, and the receptive darkness.
- The light swirl is the Yang. It is considered masculine in nature, as it represents brightness, the sun, passion, and growth.
- Despite the appearance of each half, they are considered complements, not opposites.
- Neither is superior or inferior.
- They are contradictory and yet inseparable.

In the Eastern world of philosophy, religion, and spiritual beliefs, the idea of the connectedness of all beings comes to fruition in the Ying Yang symbol.

## Calling Upon the Tao via Sacred Art

There are many things we may love about a particular philosophy. Some become part of us, and others we have to keep reading about or practicing through meditation until they become more natural. But in general, essential philosophical principles are most helpful when they are at the ready, so that you can call upon them right on the spot. This is often achieved when we visualize familiar symbols to help us connect with a certain way of thinking or being. We can do this when we have to make decisions, when we need to relax, or if we have to come up with an inspiring idea.

Aesthetics is another important branch of philosophy. It is centered primarily on art and its corollary, beauty. But art in this instance is mostly in the form of symbols.

The Yin Yang is a powerful symbol because it embodies the Tao and is a strong reminder of the inherent balance of Taoism—and that this balance is available any time.

Sometimes a very simple symbol can remind us of a great deal of philosophical information. For example, that's what a crucifix hanging in a Christian home represents. That's what the statue of Buddha or the symbol of the Endless Knot represents in a Buddhist household. If you are Taoist, or find comfort in the Taoist philosophy, it can help to have the Yin Yang symbol in your home. A simple glance reminds every Taoist of all the salient points of their philosophy. And it can make anyone feel a bit more relaxed about embracing the dualities of life.

Tibetan monks have taken the concept of Aesthetic philosophy to the highest form of expression I've ever witnessed. They are surrounded daily by countless symbolic representations. Their robes symbolize various philosophical ideas, as well as the hats that they wear and the very number of "strings" that comprise the mane of that hat. Each item they hold in their hands has symbolic meaning. Every item on a Buddhist altar has a symbolic meaning. When they make elaborate sand mandalas, every single item in that creation has symbolic meaning, and together they paint a roadmap to enlightenment. They embrace their own symbol for the interconnectedness of all being, called the Endless Knot. (You'll find a related meditation in Part Four.)

## The Importance of Contrast

According to Taoist thought, we only know things by contrast. We know happiness only because we know its opposite. The same is true for virtually everything—all things come in opposite/

complementary pairs. We only know one thing by its contrasting opposite:

- Sickness/health
- Danger/safety
- Life/death
- Ugly/beautiful

Unless something causes a reaction or makes you feel a certain way, you may not even notice it. It takes energy to notice every breath you take or every scent that wafts into your nostrils, so you just go about your day not thinking of these things—until someone leaves smelly garbage in the kitchen or you eat something that causes you to choke. That's when you notice you can't catch your breath or that you have to throw the garbage out.

That's part of the reason why you never notice a lot of things. It also explains why there are some things you can't stop noticing. When someone dies, it may cause you tremendous pain. But you feel that pain in contrast to the love and happiness you may have experienced with the person who died.

We only become aware of things, and *stay* aware of things, by contrast. And that includes what we think of (often incorrectly) as happiness. We can't be happy all the time (the way most of us think about happiness), and just like breathing in and out all day, it would cease to register without contrast.

We can only know what it means to feel powerful if we have experienced times of being downtrodden. We can only know what it means to be happy if we know what it means to be sad. You can stamp your feet all you want and say, "It just shouldn't be that way. I want to be blissfully happy all the time. I want everything to be wonderful all the time. And I never want to die." Sorry, but that isn't reality. You will be dissatisfied and frustrated forever, searching for something that doesn't exist.

## A Taoist Story

This reminds me of an old Taoist tale, which, by the way, is also told by Tibetans. It goes like this:

A poor farmer owned a horse, and one day the horse got out of its enclosure and ran away.

The neighbors said to the farmer: "What bad luck. You have lost your only horse." The farmer replied: "Bad luck. Good luck. Who can say?"

The farmer had a son who decided to go and look for the horse, and he found the horse had taken up with a beautiful wild stallion. He brought both horses back to the farmer.

Now the neighbors said: "How wise you are. You were right. It was good luck. Now you have two horses." The farmer replied: "Good luck. Bad luck. Who can say?"

The next day the son decided to break in the new horse so that they could use him to help with the farming. He got on the horse, but the horse bucked and threw him, and the son broke his leg.

The neighbors said: "Again you were right. You got a beautiful new horse, but he broke your son's leg, and now he will not be able to help you with the harvest. What bad luck!"

As you can guess, the farmer replied: "Good luck. Bad luck. Who can say?"

The next day, China went to war with Mongolia. The Mongolians were sweeping over China on horseback and killing every soldier in their path. China knew it could not win and that every soldier they sent was likely to die, but the only resource they had was their large population. So they decided to send representatives to every home to draft all the young men they found into the army, knowing they would probably be killed in the war.

When the representative got to the farmer's house, he said: "We cannot take your son. With his broken leg, he would be useless to us."

After he left, the neighbors came and said to the farmer,

"What good luck. Your son has been spared."

You can guess what the farmer said.

## Appreciating the Tao

I leave you with this thought from the *Tao Te Ching*:

*Those who wish to take the world and control it*
*I see that they cannot succeed*
*The world is a sacred instrument*
*One cannot control it*
*The one who controls it will fail*
*The one who grasps it will lose*

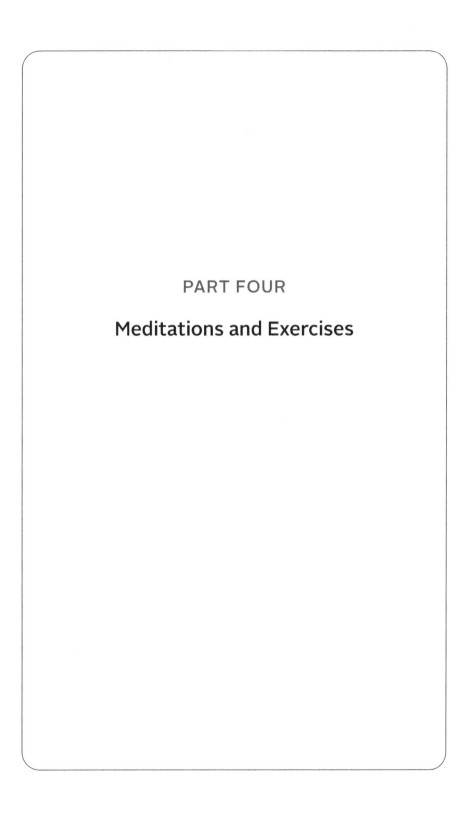

PART FOUR

# Meditations and Exercises

## CHAPTER 21

# Let's Start with Relaxation

*"Whether your stress is spiraling out of control or you've already
got it tamed, you can benefit from learning
relaxation techniques."*
— The Mayo Clinic

BEFORE YOU CAN LEARN TO meditate, you must learn to relax. And then you must learn to be still and focus. For this reason, we will begin this meditation section of the book with some basic, valuable information about your nervous system and a technique for relaxing.

There are countless reasons to learn to relax. Meditation is just one reason. Living a healthier and more peaceful life is another. Let's begin with science, specifically biology. Since this is not a medical book, I will try to keep this fairly simple.

One of the nervous systems in the body is called the Autonomic Nervous System (ANS). It controls involuntary functions in the body (like breath and heartbeat). There are two parts of the ANS: The sympathetic nervous system and the parasympathetic nervous system. In a nutshell, these two branches of the nervous system cover these bases:

- **THE SYMPATHETIC NERVOUS SYSTEM** gets the body ready for sudden stress. If you witness an accident or see someone faint suddenly, or if anything frightening occurs, it makes your heart beat faster. This sends more blood to areas in the body that may need more. It also releases adrenaline from the adrenal glands. This is meant to help you make a quick getaway if you are in danger. We commonly call this the "fight or flight" response to stressors.

- **THE PARASYMPATHETIC NERVOUS SYSTEM** does the opposite. This system is focused on preparing you for rest. It also helps the body's digestive system take in nutrients and move out what is not needed.

Let's consider our ancestor, the caveman. One day he is out hunting and sees a threat, either a wild animal or an enemy from a warring tribe. He will either decide to run away quickly or stay and fight.

- To aid in this, the sympathetic nervous system activates the fight or flight response.
- It triggers the glands to release adrenaline into his system.
- This releases cortisol, which increases his blood pressure and blood sugar.
- The heart and lungs will work harder, sending more blood to his muscles.
- It will send more energy, and this will make him stronger and faster, as well as increase his focus and vision.
- It will speed up his body's ability for blood clotting.
- It will also make him feel anxiety and/or aggression.

As his body increases in strength and energy, it shuts down non-essential functions, so all the energy used by those functions now become available for his ordeal. Among other things:

- This inhibits action in the stomach so that digestion slows down considerably or stops completely.
- The tear glands and salivary glands are inhibited (thus, dry mouth).
- Many other functions are either curtailed or stopped completely.

When the threat is over for this ancestral caveman, the parasympathetic nervous system activates his "rest and digest" system, by releasing a chemical that returns the system to balance.

## Modern-Day Cavemen and Cavewomen

While we do not necessarily run into saber-tooth tigers or troublemaking tribesmen as we walk outside our doors, our nervous systems are often besieged by perceived and actual threats. In many ways, modern humans are worse off.

In today's world we are bombarded constantly by a plethora of stresses. Some are situational (like running into a bear in the woods) and some are chronic (such as health issues, financial problems, or a caring for an elderly relative).

We have bills to pay, meetings to go to, children to raise, bosses to please, and arguments with mates. It is very easy to go from feeling your best to being stressed. This is magnified as we watch the news and hear of violence committed around the world: Acts of terrorism, school shootings, and the most recent civil unrest in this country. There is an endless parade of videos and articles showing the worst sides of human nature. Furthermore, the way we think and the kinds of things we have to think about can also make our stress long-term.

Suppose you are offered a new job with a great pay raise and more interesting work, but to take it you have to uproot your family, move to a more expensive area, find a new home to live in, look for new schools for your kids, and face a whole host of other problems and changes. This is not the kind of thing that will stress you for just a few minutes, but probably for weeks or longer.

Or, if you believe that it is important for you to "keep up with the Joneses," your stress may never end because you'll have to keep constant tabs on those Joneses and react every time they get something that you don't have. Perhaps you are jealous of the success of a colleague and spend your time trying to do better and achieve more. These kinds of thoughts and desires can keep you stressed virtually all of the time. And it's exhausting.

## Modern vs. Ancient Stress

Sadly, our nervous system does not know the difference between the kinds of stress we face today and the dangers our ancient ancestors faced. Consequently, many of us remain in a state of fight or flight, and it causes us to suffer mentally and physically.

Living in chronically stressful circumstances without any relief wreaks havoc on our nervous systems.

- Cortisol levels remain high.
- Blood pressure remains high.
- Digestion is compromised.
- We feel overwhelmed by anxiety or even aggression.

Worse still, because we never get completely into the rest and digest aspect of the cycle, we don't heal as easily as we could. The majority of healing comes when you sleep. This is why doctors always prescribe bed rest and psychologists always ask if we are getting enough sleep. Our brains and body heal during sleep. Sleep deprivation is rampant in our Western culture.

With excess adrenaline in your system, it's hard to sleep well, rest well, or heal well. You get stuck in a continuous stress cycle. If you checked your cortisol levels immediately upon awakening, you'd find they are still high, right along with your blood pressure and all the other negative side effects of not being able to relax.

So, for health reasons alone, it is well worth learning to relax, if for no other purpose than to calm and nourish the parasympathetic nervous system.

But physical health is only the beginning. Emotional and mental health is also in danger. When you are stressed out and your nervous system is out of balance, it can cause a myriad of issues.

- Creativity may be compromised. The ability to write, to draw, and even to sing and dance is weakened.
- Cognition may be compromised. You will find it much

harder to solve problems, to mediate between people, or to think straight or effortlessly.

## Relaxation Is Self-Care

It is so important to befriend your nervous system and learn to relax. Before you give to others, you must learn to be kind to yourself. This is a theme I bring up often because self-care is critical to your well-being and happiness. So much of the hope for healing our world is in finding compassion for others, yet we must first master the self-compassion that leads us to the best level of self-care.

Almost every spiritual system I have ever learned about has set forth the idea that relaxation is crucial to your well-being. Every meditation or every reflective exercise begins with learning to relax and practice relaxation.

In yoga I was taught that, of all the poses, the most important one is called shavasana, the corpse pose, where you simply lie on your back and relax. It is also described as the most difficult pose. How can lying on your back be difficult? Lying on your back is not difficult. What is difficult is learning to relax completely while you are lying there! Many people have a hard time learning to do that because they are so wired for stress. Some people struggle against it at first. Their bodies jerk in discomfort. Then, the first few times they are able to relax, they fall asleep because they need to relax *that* much.

There are many variations on relaxation exercises, but the "body scan" is one of the most common and often the most effective. This is where the importance of focus, and practicing to focus, comes in. Let's try this technique for relaxing.

## Relaxation Exercise: The Body Scan

- Lie down on a flat surface with a yoga mat or towel under you, if possible.
- Close your eyes.

- Take a few full breaths and exhalations.
- Send your mind down into your feet and start scanning from the toes up to your head, stopping at each major body part.
- Focus on each body part, notice any tension, and then allow it to release.
- First relax the feet, including the toes, then the ankles, the calves, knees, thighs, pelvis, abdomen, chest, neck, and head.

## Some things to be aware of:

**CHALLENGES.** It's not uncommon to encounter a few challenges when you first try this. You may fall asleep long before you complete the exercise. Don't worry. It will be a very valuable short nap. The more you do this exercise, the longer you will stay awake until it is not a problem staying awake for the entire time.

**ATTENTION ISSUES.** The more common problem is lack of attention. You may begin to do the exercise, relax the feet, go to your ankles, and maybe even before you get to your calves, you will lose your train of thought. Eventually you will realize that your mind has wandered and you are no longer doing the exercise.

**CRITICIZING YOURSELF.** If or when this happens the most important thing is not to get upset. Don't berate yourself. Don't get angry. Don't start an entire story about how you failed. Don't tax your brain with any negative talk. Just immediately get back to the exercise.

## Backup Plan for Beginners

If you find the full-body scans too hard at first, don't stress over it. Here are two possible solutions.

1. **FOCUS ON SPECIFIC AREAS.** Sometimes it is too much to focus on every part of the body. Try scanning a bigger body part and moving up to the other areas, covering a wider portion of your body at a time. Fewer steps make it easier to stay focused. For example, focus on scanning:

   - Your feet and ankles all at once
   - The entire leg
   - The entire chest and abdominal area
   - The neck and face together

2. **TRY GUIDED MEDITATION.** The best choice for beginners is a guided meditation. You can also record it yourself. Most of us have smart phones with the ability to record our voices. You can even download free music, if you want to get creative, you can record the steps of the exercise as if you were guiding somebody else. Here are some tips:

   - Speak every step slowly, from start to finish.
   - Relay what body part to focus on.
   - Say when it is time to recognize tension.
   - Indicate when to relax the muscles.

Once you've done this, you'll have a recording you can play for yourself to guide you through the exercise. But if you would rather have a more experienced voice lead you through, there are many options for this kind of relaxation that work well. They are available through a variety of apps. Often you can find what you need on YouTube.com. Look for "guided meditation" or "relaxation meditation."

By far the most important thing is to learn to relax. So don't stress over any of this. Do the best you can, and before long you will be able to relax.

Next, we will look at the mechanics of meditation.

# CHAPTER 22

# How to Meditate

*"Meditation is like a gym in which you develop the powerful
mental muscles of calm and insight."*
— *Ajahn Brahm*

THROUGH MEDITATION, WE CAN CULTIVATE the spirit and learn about ourselves. It offers a connection to the world and an understanding of our connection to others. There are many different types of meditation, each with a specific focus.

The purpose of mediation is to allow you to focus inwardly and learn how your own mind works. As discussed in the last chapter, it is important to practice the art of relaxing and focusing. These are keys to beginning your meditation practice.

You will learn a great deal about yourself, and as we have discussed throughout this book, self-awareness is the key to personal and planetary transformation. Mediation is a core technique that will allow you to cultivate the Virtues of the Heart outlined in Section Two of this book. It will also help you try some of the meditations that follow this chapter.

It may seem strange when you first start, but once you get into the groove of your own meditation practice, it will actually make you feel better, clearer, and happier. Meditation all by itself is relaxing. Whether you use guided meditation or learn to adapt your own techniques, you will certainly feel more relaxed than you did before you started.

Here are some basic mechanics of meditation that will help you create a safe space for your meditation practice.

## Sacred Environment

I have a friend who could only meditate in the bathtub, when her baby was asleep. Another friend always sits in a comfy chair in her living room near a statue of Buddha, to help her focus. Another has a full meditation room in her home that has music and a Tibetan singing bowl.

Create a space in your home or designate an area where you won't be disturbed, so that you can invest time in sitting quietly and alone. It is best to have a place in your home where you can find some peace, even if it is the bathroom or laundry room. Try going there at the same time each day to start developing a new habit. Begin with five minutes and then ten, and work your way to longer meditations.

You can also learn to do walking meditations by taking a walk in the neighborhood, a park, or along a beach.

Meditation doesn't have to be drawn out, and the environment does not have to be fancy. All you need to succeed is within you.

## Anchoring

There is a technique from Neuro-Linguistic Programming called anchoring, in which you connect an internal state to an external physical gesture. There are many you can use, but let me suggest a few for you that I use. Feel free to choose or add your own.

Once you are relaxed:

- Put your palms together, facing up, with one hand on top of the other. You can start by putting one palm on your lap, then put the other on top of it.
- Take your thumb and middle finger of one hand and

    encircle the wrist of the other hand. Then squeeze the wrist gently and say to yourself (silently or out loud), "Relax."

- Or place both hands on your lap with palms facing up and place your thumbs and middle fingers together and silently say to yourself, "Relax."

I have done this kind of anchoring over time, and it has become a shortcut to my "on switch." When I am stressed, I can simply repeat one of these anchors (and say "Relax"), and it will relax me immediately. Of course, it is not quite as effective as going through the entire exercise, but it sure works well on the spot.

## Meditating Without Prompts

Although you may use guided meditation at first, eventually you will want to learn to do this without a recording, using only your mind to guide you through the exercise. This is because the second thing we want to build up is our ability to focus. It's no use learning the greatest exercises in the world if, ten seconds into it, your mind strays and you forget what you are doing. So the next exercise is to build your ability to focus.

## Cultivating Attention

There are many different exercises that are used to cultivate attention. The primary variation among them is exactly what to focus on. I have chosen the breath. This is so common that virtually every form of meditation includes it at some point, and most begin with this exercise.

One of the reasons that I have chosen breath as a focus is because you always have it with you. Your breath is always available to you, and it is inconspicuous. Nobody needs to know that you are doing an exercise.

The other reason that many traditions use the breath as a focus is because it is the gateway between the conscious and the unconscious. It is the bridge between the voluntary and the involuntary. Under normal circumstances, breathing is automatic. Whether you are asleep or even unconscious, your breathing continues. But you *can* take control of your breathing. That is one of the reasons that disciplines like yoga focus on breath exercises, or as they call them, pranayama. Here we are concerned only with increasing your ability to focus. Before we begin the breathing exercises, let's talk about some essential factors.

- **LEARN TO BREATHE CORRECTLY.** You may think it odd that one needs to learn to breathe, but most people do not breathe correctly. Many breathe through their mouth, which has numerous drawbacks. Passing air through the nostrils serves several purposes, such as filtering out dust and warming the air before it is sent to your lungs.

- **PAY ATTENTION TO PHYSIOLOGY.** Secondly, many people (especially those with military experience) are told to suck in the stomach and thrust out their chest. This is *not* a good way to breathe and drastically cuts down the amount of air you can take in.

- **USE YOUR NOSE.** The first rule of meditative breathing is to breathe in and out through the nostrils and not the mouth. Breathing in and out through our nostrils also increases oxygen to our brain.

- **RELAX YOUR STOMACH.** The second rule is to allow your diaphragm to do the breathing. To test that you are doing it correctly, put some light item, even a piece of paper, on your abdomen. As you breathe in and out, you should see the item on your stomach rise and fall as you breathe.

## Concentration Exercise: The Breath

1. It is important to relax before you do any meditation, so start every meditation you do by settling in comfortably, either in some cross-legged posture on the floor or a cushion, or simply sitting in a chair with your feet on the ground.

It's important to keep the posture erect, but not rigidly at attention. Just tell yourself to relax, or if you have time, you can do a full-body scan. If you've been practicing anchoring, you can also use your anchor to assist you in relaxing. Once you feel comfortable, you are ready to proceed.

2.  Now take a few relaxing breaths. You are *not* trying to influence or control your breath. You are not aiming for any particular speed or depth of breathing. However, you will soon find that even when you don't consciously try to control your breathing, the mere fact of bringing attention to the breath will make your breath tend to slow down and deepen. That's okay. Just don't make an effort to intentionally do anything to the breath. This is called a "natural" breath.

3.  Once you have established a natural breath, we begin the task of counting breaths. You can begin the count on the inhale or the exhale. Different schools have differing opinions as to which you should use, but in this case, it really doesn't matter.

4.  Let's use the outbreath this time. Breathe in, and then when you breathe out, count "one" silently to yourself.

5.  Continue breathing and on the next outbreath count "two" and so on.

The object (eventually) is to be able to count to ten. You may be amazed to find that you cannot do it. When I started, I could not even get to three!

You may begin counting, and before you know it, you find that your mind has wandered off somewhere else and you are no longer counting. This is normal, so don't be concerned.

Although we are training our attention span, this is not the thing to focus on. It is far more important to learn to be kind to yourself. Self-care is key. So if your mind wanders, don't beat yourself up over it or talk to yourself about it. Simply start over again immediately without any mental conversation or negative emotional feelings.

Try the exercise for as long as it seems relaxing to you.

If you begin to get bothered or uncomfortable with the exercise, simply stop for now and try again later or tomorrow. Gradually your attention will increase, and eventually you will have no problem counting to ten or almost any other number.

## Alternative Breathing Exercise

If one technique doesn't work, or work at first, there is always another approach that may be a bit less complex. As alternatives to just counting breaths as described above, you can try one or all of the following ideas:

- **BE AWARE OF IT.** Simply become aware of the breath. "Watch" it as your breath comes in and goes down into your lungs, and then comes back up again and out your nostrils.
- **FEEL IT.** Focus on the feeling of the breath at the tip of the nostrils as it comes in and goes out.
- **ALTERNATE APPROACHES.** You can also choose to alternate among the three approaches. Count your breaths, watch the breath coming in and out, and focus on the feeling at the nostrils.

When I say alternate, I don't mean you have to do that in any particular order. You may be feeling the breath at the nostrils, and then when you realize you've lost your focus, start to count the breaths, which brings back focus. Then if you lose count, relax a bit by simply watching the breath. By switching back and forth, you can do this exercise far longer than if you only used one method.

## Exercise for Insomniacs

People tell me all the time that they are suffering from insomnia and at a loss for finding a way to get good rest. Breathing exercises can help!

People who have insomnia can try the following:

- Focus on your breath.
- Visualize the numbers one through ten in the middle of your forehead.
- Visualize the number one and breathe.
- Visualize the number two and breathe—and so on.
- Keep going until number ten, if you are still awake.
- If that doesn't work, reverse it and start with: 10, 9, 8, 7, 6, 5, 4, 3, 2, and 1.

In the next chapters we will learn new meditations and new ways to meditatively reflect on important issues.

# CHAPTER 23

# Reflecting on the Endless Knot Exercise

*"The idea of interdependence is central to Buddhism, which holds that all things come into being through the mutual interactions of various causes and conditions."*
— Daisaku Ikeda

BUDDHISTS BELIEVE THAT WE ARE all tied together, that we are all connected. It isn't enough to just seek your own happiness or refrain from impeding someone else from seeking their happiness. We need to actively strive to help each other attain happiness in order to attain our own happiness.

The symbol that represents our interconnectedness is known in the Buddhist tradition as the Endless Knot. It intertwines upon itself with no beginning and no end. The unbroken and interwoven cord represents love and a connectedness to all things. It is a culmination and representation of so many of the things I have presented in this book.

It also represents the balance of pairs:

- The intertwining of wisdom and compassion
- The mutual dependence of the religious doctrine and secular affairs
- The union of wisdom and method
- The inseparability of emptiness and dependent arising
- The union of wisdom, and compassion of enlightenment

## A Case for Helping Strangers

Perhaps you feel that you don't really have anything in common with the strangers that you are supposed to help along the way to your own happiness. If so, I urge you to reconsider.

In this chapter we will review some of the concepts we've discussed in the book before we proceed to the reflection exercise at the end.

The entire world is made up of people building things together, from communities to the chair you are sitting in. Look around your own living room. Can you spot a single thing that was not made or provided by someone else? Even if your spouse designed the chair you are sitting on and hammered it together with his or her own hands, the wood, nails, and other parts came from someone else. Even your own body and the millions of molecules that constitute it come from your mother and father, who inherited from their mothers and fathers, who inherited it from their ancestors.

This is true for everyone. Our mutual reliance on each other and the fact that we share this amazing planet makes us more interconnected than we realize. It is something we all fundamentally have in common.

Let me refer back to the Lesson of the Pencil, which is a powerful example we discussed earlier. The economist Milton Friedman illustrated the idea in the context of the economy. Essentially, every aspect of a pencil is imported from a different place in the world. It literally takes thousands of people to get the pencil made and to make it available to you in a store. These people may never know each other or see each other, nor do they all speak the same language or live in the same environment. Yet together, they collaborated to make the pencil that sits on your desk.

Just as the Endless Knot represents the interdependence of all who share this earth, the Lesson of the Pencil also shows us we are dependent on one another.

## We Are All Connected

In this modern era, we often think we are self-sufficient individuals, separate from a greater whole. We often view ourselves as independent, unique, different, and unbound by the actions and decision of others.

That is not the reality of our lives, however. People have had to rely on other people since the beginning of time. This holds true for relationships as well as goods and services. The more modern and high-tech we become, the more connected we are. There is not a single thing or person in existence that does not depend on others to exist. Even our thoughts are born of others' thoughts. Without language, there is no thought. Someone had to invent language. It is impossible to exist without being connected to the history of humanity.

Buddhists say we are connected to all beings, not just humans. On a scientific level that is clearly true. We are all made up of different combinations of the same building blocks of life—carbon, nitrogen, hydrogen, oxygen. Therefore, we are quite literally all related. Bill Bryson wrote a wonderful book called *A Short History of Nearly Everything,* which goes into great scientific detail on the topic.

If we can agree, through these various examples, that we are truly interconnected, how can we apply that knowledge to our lives and our shared search for happiness? Acknowledging our connection to others is a good first step. Compassion for others is the next step to attaining our own fundamental happiness.

## The Endless Knot of Happiness

Buddhists believe that all beings (not just humans) have a desire to be happy and deserve to be happy. But what is happiness? For some people, the immediate answer may be wealth, success, beauty, or health, but those things are impermanent and fleeting.

The Buddhist idea of impermanence states that nothing is

forever. You can lose your wealth, health, or success. Those things may bring temporary joy, but joy is not the same as happiness, which abides regardless of circumstances. It may sound trite, but it is true that happiness comes from within.

Can you think of any one thing, person, or situation that unfailingly brings you happiness all the time? Some things to consider:

- Happiness does not come from any external person or thing—it is possible for anyone to attain.
- Think of all the time and energy you invest in trying to control external circumstances and the accumulation of material objects in your life.
- Do you spend anywhere near this amount of time and energy on inner development, such as introspection, cultivating self-discipline, or thinking altruistically of others?
- How much time do you spend on the spiritual pursuit of such things as meditation, prayer, and reflection?
- Decide now to try to develop greater happiness and fulfillment through balancing outer activities with inner development.

## Step Off the Road to Unhappiness

In general, we tend to focus on the short-term and not think about the long-term consequences of our actions. We place entirely too much value on external, material circumstances, while undervaluing or sometimes ignoring our internal cognitive processes. We focus on narrow self-interest at the expense of a broader worldview. These habits can keep us from understanding that we are part of the Endless Knot. That is why we have to consider developing new habits and a new approach to the search for happiness by including the success and well-being of others in the equation.

## Start a Gratitude List

In order to share happiness and spread it through compassion, you must experience happiness first. A simple, time-honored approach is to start with gratitude. Research has shown that gratitude improves outlook on life. Writing down what you are grateful for is especially powerful.

Write your own list. To get you started, here are some basic aspects of life to be grateful for:

- If you have food in the refrigerator, clothes on your back, a roof over your head, and a place to sleep, you are "richer" than 75 percent of the population on this planet.
- If you own a computer with internet service, you are part of the 1 percent in the world who does.
- If you woke up with more good health than illness, you are more fortunate than the thousands who will not even survive this day.
- If you have never experienced the fear of battle, the loneliness of imprisonment, the agony of torture, or the pangs of starvation, you are better off than 700 million people in this world.
- If you can attend the place of worship of your choice without the fear of harassment, arrest, torture, or death, you are more blessed than three billion people in this world.

Your gratitude list can also include all the great things that happen in life, such as landing a job interview or getting a great new babysitter. It should celebrate the simple pleasures, such as receiving a beautiful greeting card or text that makes you smile. Keep adding things you are grateful for, every day, even if they seem small and inconsequential. Every drop of gratitude adds to your happiness.

We are so blessed to have the exceptional good fortune of being alive in this moment. Gratitude is the antidote to all forms of despair. But it requires a shift in our habitual thinking to recognize that outside forces are not responsible for our inner feelings.

## The Gift of Being Human

Buddhists cultivate compassion through study and meditation. Compassion Meditation involves silently repeating certain phrases that express intention to move from judgment to caring, from isolation to connection, from indifference to understanding. Here is a short analytical meditation on the gift of being human that you can practice daily:

- **REFLECT ON ALL LIVING THINGS.** There are hundreds of thousands of species, some still unknown to man. Consider how rare it is to be born human. And rarer still to be blessed with the time and ability to pursue happiness.

- **THINK TO YOURSELF:** "I have an opportunity to learn to practice the techniques of compassion. I am grateful for all my gifts. May I learn to use this to help others be happy."

Shifting the focus from yourself to others will create happiness for you, as well as others. Take the first step toward celebrating the connection of all beings and taking your place in the Endless Knot of life.

## CHAPTER 24

# Walk in Someone Else's Shoes Meditation

*"Whenever you are about to find fault with someone, ask yourself
the following question: What fault of mine most nearly resembles
the one I am about to criticize?"*
— Marcus Aurelius

I BELIEVE THE ISSUES THAT CHALLENGE and divide
our world are moral issues. We must reflect on our behavior
and actions. We must be willing to uproot our prejudices and
acknowledge the privileges that we came into the world with—
and how they drive certain attitudes and beliefs. Assess whether
they are helping or hurting the community. Taking positive action
is imperative. Doing so peacefully is also important. Violence is
never the answer for making change. The more we strive to understand
one another, the healthier our world will be.

This exercise is to help you connect with your empathic nature
to get a sense of the reality of others around you and to enable you
to connect authentically with people of all backgrounds.

## Prepare for the Meditation

We start all meditations with calming and centering for a few
moments by taking a few deep breaths and relaxing. Then we
consciously think about what we are about to do so that we can
do it mindfully. We think about the nature of the practice we are

about to engage in, and remind ourselves of the purpose of the exercise. In this case, we remind ourselves that we are trying to cultivate empathy.

## Meditate on Who You Are

Think about your life.

- Call to mind the joys and the challenges, but focus on the best parts of being you.
- Do you have a great love life, career, or home? Is your neighborhood nice? Are there people who love you? Do you have money for food and shelter? Focus on what is good about your life and about who you are.
- Now imagine what it would be like if you were born as someone else, in a less fortunate situation.

There are so many ways that your life *could* have been much more difficult—and you would not have had any choice about those circumstances.

Surely you would have been a very different person had you grown up in a different time, as a different sex, in different financial circumstances, in a different country, under a different form of government, or into a race, religion, or tribe that is persecuted and suffering.

You may have experienced suffering in your life and have relatives who have as well. But if you have liberties, food to eat, and a place to live, you are in a better position than so many others in our world. The United Nations reports that as we sit down to our meals each day, there are:

- A billion children living in poverty
- More than 1.3 billion people who live on less than $1.25 a day
- 850 million people who do not have enough food to eat
- 750 million people who lack adequate access to clean drinking water

As sad as these harsh realities may be, take a moment to recognize that terrible hardships exist for so many. Suffering runs deep. Individuals who have had ancestors who were enslaved, killed, or wrongfully forced to leave their land still suffer. People fleeing war, violence, ethnic cleansing, communism, dictators, and all levels of diaspora are still a reality today. They flee on foot or by boat, climb fences, and encounter all kinds of dangers in their desperation to get their families to safety.

So if you were born in a country where you are a citizen who receives national benefits, you are in in a much better place than people who have no home, rights, or means to survive.

Think about some of those people who are suffering, the ones you have seen on the news. They are human beings with the same humanity as you and your family, but they were born into less fortunate circumstances.

That alone should encourage you to be more compassionate for those not as lucky as you. In fact, you may feel terrible for those who have suffered, and you may even take action to help them.

But what about the people whom you do not like or agree with? What about the people you think are bad? Can you find compassion for them too?

This is what it really means to "walk in someone else's shoes."

## Meditate on a Difficult Person

Hate is a very strong word and people use it too freely. Certain people seem unworthy of any empathy, especially if they do not offer empathy. Some people are cruel and narcissistic, and everything they do hurts others. You may not want to walk in their shoes. But I invite you to try.

- Pick one person you perceive as a personal nemesis, a public danger, or anyone you consider a "difficult person."
- Let their image come to mind.
- Allow yourself to feel the feelings associated with them—

mistrust, anger, upset, fear, disruption, or whatever they bring up in you.

- Now sit with this discomfort for 60 seconds. Now for another 60 seconds.
- Allow yourself to name the discomfort so you are clear about the emotions this person evokes.
- Consider if there is anything this person does that reminds you of something in you, particularly a trait you find less than favorable—such as being too pushy, greedy, moody, disorganized, inauthentic, or whatever else comes up.
- Consider if there is anything this person does that triggers pain or memories, or unidentified discomfort, that may be related to someone who has hurt or abused you in the past.
- Try to acknowledge these things without judgment or self-judgment, as it is just another way to look at why some people upset us and drive us crazy.
- Come out of this uncomfortable moment by taking three deep breaths and following each with a deep, releasing breath.

You may discover that this person who disturbs you somehow holds a mirror to your own behavior, or triggers fear related to people who have hurt you. Awareness of these facts is beneficial to your personal growth. Recognizing that some difficult people grate on us because they trigger something inside us is powerful. This helps us take control by recognizing our own responsibility for how we react.

And if we treat ourselves compassionately in this process, it also allows us to see the difficult person from a different point of view. If we are able to see that we are responding from our own inner reactions based on our own influences and pain, perhaps we can see that the difficult person is doing the same.

## Meditate on Empathy

We all have complex lives, and there are many things that make us who we are and cause us to react in certain ways. Just as you have explored your own feelings and reactions related to a difficult person, now is the time to explore how you might react if you *were* that person. This is to help you truly walk in their shoes.

Bring the difficult person back into your mind. Take a moment to imagine the complexity of causes that add to who they are and how they conduct themselves. If this is a public person, you can research more about their background. Maybe you know some of the essentials about this person because they are part of your community or family. You may be aware of their traumas, losses, regrets, failures and pain. Perhaps you know this person has gone through a grueling divorce, lost a loved one to drug abuse, or lost their business or job. Maybe you are aware they had controlling parents or parents who paid no attention, or that they lost a parent to suicide. There may be a million different things that add to the way they behave and present themselves in the world.

You may not ever know all the factors that make them who they are or make them "difficult," but call to mind whatever you do know. And then think of yourself in the same situation.

Ask yourself, what would life be like for you if you had the same "causes" or influences as the difficult person has in their life? For example, how would your life have turned out if some of the following things had occurred?

- You had all the same losses and disappointments.
- You had the same parents.
- You had the same genes as this person.
- You were born in the same year.
- You came from the same place and culture.
- Your parents treated you exactly as they treated this person.
- You had the same kinds of relationships and friendships.
- You had the same early childhood traumas.
- You had the same kind of rejections and prejudice.
- You had the same health and mental health issues.
- You had a painful experience you never healed from.

## Absorb and Contemplate

If you had *all* of the same experiences as this person and were influenced by the same things that influenced their behavior, it is likely that you would act just as they do. This is not to say that your awareness will influence their behavior. It means you have the ability to understand this person more clearly through your willingness to empathize. That can be a powerful catalyst for healing.

We can never change others, or expect them to change. But we can always change our behavior and our reactions to others. We can lead by example.

## Benefiting Yourself and the Planet

I hope this gets you thinking. And doing. Do as little or as much as you can, but do *something* to make a small change. Don't wait for others to do it. Have the courage, perseverance, and determination to live your authentic life. The world will benefit—because when everyone takes responsibility for themselves and their behavior, this planet is a better place to be.

Remember most of all: The best thing you can do for yourself and your own benefit is to be good to others. Help people as much as you can. And, as much as possible, love others. And if you still can't feel the love, consider sending good energy their way by making a wish for their well-being and happiness.

# CHAPTER 25

# Metta Meditation

*"Metta can only be founded in its most sympathetic and authentic
form when it comes from the most humble
and truest of intentions."*
— Amy Leigh Mercree

METTA MEDITATION IS ONE OF the most important
meditations in the Tibetan Buddhist tradition because
it addresses all of the Four Virtues of the Heart, which
we discussed in detail in Chapters 7 and 8. It teaches compassion
and loving kindness with the goal of eliminating fear. Practicing
this meditation on a regular basis can change your life. It can also
change the world.

Tradition has it that the Buddha first taught Metta meditation
as an antidote to fear. The story goes that he sent a group of
monks to meditate in a forest. The monks, according to the story,
soon learned that the trees were inhabited by terrifying spirits.
They quickly fled from the forest. They begged the Buddha to
send them to meditate somewhere else—anywhere but that forest!
Buddha told them that he was going to send them right back into
the same forest. "But this time," he said, "I'm going to give you
protection." And then he taught the Metta meditation for the first
time. He encouraged the monks to recite certain phrases (which
follow below). But, he told them, it was not enough to merely

recite the phrases, they had to acquire a heartfelt feeling for loving-kindness.

The tree spirits were so moved by the feelings of loving-kindness generated by the monks that they decided to serve and protect the monks. Legend or not, the moral and meaning of the story are what matters: We can penetrate fear with loving-kindness. If fear arises, it need not overpower your mind.

All meditations start with relaxation, so sit comfortably and relax. Close your eyes and focus on your breath. As the Buddha would say, "Be at ease." Now, think of at least one thing that you really like about yourself and spend just a few moments thinking about these qualities within you.

Start this meditation by silently saying to yourself:

**May I be free from danger.**
**May I be happy.**
**May I be healthy.**
**May I live with ease.**

Keep in mind that by danger, we mean all kinds of danger, internal as well as external. "May I live with ease" refers to all the ordinary experiences of daily life. Imagine that your daily life will go easily, and not be a struggle. Each phrase should come from your heart, using the power of intention.

As you say these phrases together, develop a rhythm for yourself:

**May I be free from danger.**
**May I be happy.**
**May I be healthy.**
**May I live with ease.**

If you find your thoughts wandering, don't worry; just bring your attention gently back. Next, we expand these wishes to other beings. Traditionally, the first person to whom we expand this is called "the benefactor." This is someone who has been good to you and cared for you. (This was first discussed in Chapter 7).

Now remember the good that this person has done for you, and offer them loving-kindness through the phrases:

**May you be free from danger.**
**May you be happy.**
**May you be healthy.**
**May you live with ease.**

Next, we direct the intentions to a really good friend. So think of a good friend, say their name, and use your power of good intention on them: **May you be free from danger. May you be happy. May you be healthy. May you live with ease.**

The next person is the one we call the neutral person. Somebody you know, but you have neutral feelings for them: **May you be free from danger. May you be happy. May you be healthy. May you live with ease.**

Now it's time for us to move on to a difficult person. Somebody who is mildly difficult, annoying, or irritating to you. Picture this person in your mind and say: **May you be free from danger. May you be happy. May you be healthy. May you live with ease.**

Gradually we work to incorporate more and more difficult people. I am not saying that you need to forgive these people right now or to feel deep love for them. It's about recognizing oneness—the fact that we are not really separate. Offering kindness to someone like this does not make you weak—it makes you a human being who has a magnificent capacity to love. Love is our greatest strength. So you say to this person: **May you be free from danger. May you be happy. May you be healthy. May you live with ease.**

And finally, we extend our wishes to all living beings: **May all beings be free from danger. May they be happy. May they be healthy. May they live with ease.**

Now open your eyes, and remember to take your meditation experience back with you into the world of your daily life. Remember to wish all beings loving-kindness, and remember to love, honor, and respect yourself. **May you be free from danger. May you be happy. May you be healthy. May you live with ease.**

Metta is unconditional. It is simply a gift with no expectations and presented with loving-kindness. If a person does something that might disappoint, the feeling of loving-kindness still remains.

Metta is not about putting on a happy face and always pretending that everything is great. It is not about simply accepting abuse and repressing our feelings of pain or anger. It is not about accepting things or actions which are morally wrong. Having a loving heart is not about living behind a mask.

Cultivating compassion attempts to open our minds. It teaches us to embrace the pleasures and the pains of everyday life and to be completely authentic—for ourselves and for others.

Extending love and compassion to people we don't particularly like can be the trickiest part of Buddhism and the Metta meditation for some people, because we tend to hold grudges and resentments. Most of us have no trouble extending good wishes to people we like or even those whom we are neutral about, but it may seem odd being nice to terrible people who hurt others or are proponents of hatred.

It is easy to cut those people out of the equation, because they are difficult and we may feel powerless or resistant to change them. But practicing love and compassion toward them is actually the very best thing to do.

Buddhism teaches that we must practice sending good wishes to those we perceive as bad, mean, or unworthy, in the same way we would practice a new skill or try to achieve a new goal. Troubled and difficult people are often the ones who truly need compassion and love.

So, in sending our love and compassion to the difficult people, we hope that our love can act as the seed for them to develop their Buddha nature. Wishing good things for all is the same as wishing for a world where all people are good. Leading by example is the only way to enact change.

Those of us who have much to give have a responsibility to make a difference in the world. But even the poorest of poor can give love and compassion. We are all compassionate beings. Buddhism provides a number of ways in which to practice compassion and love for ourselves and others.

# CHAPTER 26

# Wave Exercise

*"Look past your thoughts, so you may drink
the pure nectar of This Moment."*
— *Rumi*

THIS FINAL MEDITATION IS BRIEF but important. It is about understanding the nature of the mind, thoughts, and keeping focus during meditation.

All meditation comes back to mindfulness. Mindfulness is defined as becoming aware of what is happening, while it is happening, without prejudice. Prejudice is a synonym for judgment. In meditation, we are trying to learn how to see things and not judge them. Our perceptions and bias tend to distort the moment, making it hard to be in the moment.

So take a moment to breathe in deeply and release your breath on a strong exhale. Sometimes it helps to release your breath on a long sigh, imagining all prejudice and negativity leaving you with the sigh.

Anchor yourself by putting your hands in your lap, palms facing upward. This is also seen as a way to receive good energy during your meditation.

Clear your mind as you place your feet firmly on the ground, to better center yourself.

Think about the nature of the meditation practice you have

been embarking on. Perhaps this book is a refresher or perhaps all the information is brand-new. You have been working with your heart, soul, mind, and breath. You have been exploring ways to cultivate the Virtues of the Heart and ways in which you can be a more compassionate person. You've done so much inner work, and I hope you feel proud and perhaps more confident. It could be that meditating is becoming easier and more natural. If not, every time you practice, you will be more comfortable.

The following is a combination of meditation and education on how to use this experience to understand how thoughts flow into your mind.

## Meditate

When you feel relaxed, centered, and ready, allow the meditation to begin with a visualization.

Imagine you are on the beach. You are sitting on the sand watching the ocean ebb and flow to and from the shore. You notice waves getting bigger, and then getting smaller. Then their pattern seems choppy and irregular. Notice where your eye goes in this visualization, as the waves continue to move. Where does your mind go? Does it flit from wave to shore, from the long view of the ocean to the water turning sand into mud at the shore? Or does it focus on one wave pattern, as it tumbles and folds?

Now stop for a moment and give some thought to where the meditation took you. Do you feel peaceful or a little uneasy? Do you feel frustrated by the constant, unpredictable movement of the water? Whatever you feel, just make a note of it. This first part is only an exercise in seeing how the mind wanders.

## Waves Are a Metaphor

Here's an explanation of why waves are used as a visualization or metaphor in meditation. There are many lessons in this procedure:

- The waves are disturbances on top of the ocean.

- They are distracting and pull your attention in different directions.
- But the waves are only the surface.
- What exists below them is calm water.
- And this calm water is everywhere and in everything,
- Beneath the waves is the true nature of what you are seeing—and the same applies to your mind!

## Discover the Underlying Stillness

All of those thoughts that are running through your mind are like the waves on the water. They are simply ripples in your mind. The underlying stillness that lies beneath them is the true nature of your mind. With mindfulness we aim to get past the frenetic thoughts, which, like waves, can distract us or lead us away from the calm waters below.

The object is *not* to try to stop our thoughts. You can no more stop your thoughts than you can stop the waves on the ocean. The object is not to stop them. The idea is to not to get caught up in them and to judge them, or talk to yourself about them (which in and of itself is a judgment). When the mind chatters during meditation think of it as waves on the ocean. They are just hanging around on the surface and dancing to the shore, but the still water is beneath. If you were below the surface, all you would see is calm water.

## Practice the Meditation Again

Bring yourself back to the ocean and try the meditation at the top of this chapter. This time, go beyond the shore and ride past the waves. Even if you get bumped around, or have waves crashing around you, be brave. Go further, in your visualization, past the rising and falling waters, past the loud crashing waves, and past the chaotic dance of the ocean. Go, deeper now, to the quiet part. Stay there, knowing you are safe and secure. Be there in the silent, calm stillness of sea. Rest there. If the waves start making noise again, acknowledge them and go back to the stillness. Know that the stillness is always there for you. Know that the silence is always there for you. Know that you can reach this delicious state by just calling it to mind.

## Improve Your Focus

How do you feel now? A little calmer? Less rattled? At peace with the ocean?

It takes practice, so don't worry if you are still battling those waves on your first tries. The waves are ever-present, as is the stillness. It's just a matter of where you put your focus.

The object is to learn that there is a vast body of calm water below the waves of your mind. With time, you can learn to access that part of yourself on a regular basis. You will become more skillful and confident.

And that's why the translation of the word for this kind of meditation in Tibetan is Shamatha. Shamatha may often be described as "focus" but the actual translation of the word is "calm abiding." So you are learning to rest your mind; to put your mind at ease and to cease endless judgment, which is represented by the waves.

PART FIVE

# Putting It All Together

# CHAPTER 27

# Feed Your Body, Mind, and Spirit

*"Take time to feed your soul and keep
the mind-body-spirit connection strong."*
— Dee Waldeck

W E'VE COVERED A LOT OF ground in this book, and
I hope it has given you many options to think about. I
hope it has offered insight that helps you understand the
underlying personal philosophy you have been guided by and also
inspires you to add new aspects and traditions that sing to you.

Most importantly, please be sure to be kind to yourself and
to find time for yourself. Daily meditation should not be a chore
but a gift you are giving yourself. Consider it to be your special
time. Self-care is your sacred privilege, and everything you do to
help yourself is important. It adds healing to our world when one
individual takes care of himself or herself and chooses to live a
life of self-love and self-awareness.

A theme that has been a major focus of this book has been
doing things that cultivate the Virtues of the Heart. And there are
ways to do this without being spiritual or becoming a Buddhist.
This is one of the reasons I believe these virtues can help *anyone*
of any background and ultimately can help all humanity.

In large measure, the virtues deal with caring about others,
but they also strongly guide you to care about yourself. Self-

compassion and compassion for others are inextricably linked. Self-compassion begins with taking care of yourself and nurturing your body, mind, and spirit.

The Virtues of the Heart teach us to focus on feelings for others and to tune into others and understand what they are dealing with. Meditation and mindfulness are ways to slow down and center yourself. They are tools for getting beyond the waves of thoughts and connecting with a quiet place within.

Life is so crazy these days, and everything moves so fast. When we are engaged in life, we are busy—but sometimes we become too busy. And the activities cut us off from self-awareness.

- When your body or your mind are moving too fast, you can't see and feel all that is happening.
- When you can't feel everything, your heart can become indifferent or numb.
- When you become numb, you then tune out others and the world.
- When you tune out the world, you disconnect.

The importance of self-awareness is that it helps you reconnect, at any moment. It helps you get back on track. And it also helps you recognize that you function at your best when you are relaxed. You are at your most sincere in that state and, by the way, you are also in the optimum condition for health.

Take some time to slow down for some portion of every day of your life. Even if you don't meditate, take time to contemplate and reflect. Take time to breathe. Take time for you.

## Address Your Own Needs

Take care of yourself on every level. Let your mind rest in a state of gratitude for what is.

- There are many things that can and do happen in life that are not exactly wonderful, but there are many more that are indeed wonderful.

- There are an endless amount of life events, opportunities, experiences, and people that make us feel grateful.
- There is a beautiful world out there. Despite the pain and sadness, there is greatness and beauty.
- Every day, if you give it some thought, I bet you can come up with five things for which to express gratitude. Write them down.

Your life will be infinitely better if you focus more on the wonderful things in life than the bad things. Do not be swayed into negativity or blinded by the darkness. Even darkness is not what it seems.

The word "dark" is a code word that scientists use to convey that they know nothing about dark energy and matter. And yet, dark matter and dark energy make up approximately 95 percent of the universe. This tells us that at best, everything we know about the universe is limited to a maximum of about 4 percent of what there is to know. This means about 5 percent represents our entire history of the acquisition of knowledge. So we don't even know all there is to know. We haven't seen all there is to see. We don't have enough insight into the vast planet and universe we inhabit to truly judge that everything is dark in a bad way.

This means we live in an incredibly fantastic place. There are so many things for us to be grateful for and to learn.

Life and the universe are a miracle on virtually every level, from the microcosm to the macrocosm. Your brain has 100 billion neurons and 125 trillion synapses. The universe contains one billion trillion stars. Light can travel 186,000 miles in a single second, yet it would take a light beam at least 83 billion years to go from one end to the other of the known and visible universe.

So focus on being grateful to be here. If you begin to see the universe as a living, breathing miracle, it will be easier to see yourself that way. And then you can see others that way. We each hold a piece of the puzzle, and when we interlock our pieces together through compassion, we all become whole.

## Nourish Yourself on All Levels

You exist in this world on so many levels, and you must honor all of them.

**TAKE CARE OF YOUR BODY.** One of the principal differences between living beings and all other things is movement. Dead things are inanimate, so keep moving to help you stay alive. Eat the best food you can manage. Every time you eat, be grateful that you have something to eat.

**FEED YOUR MIND.** Learn as much as you can at all times. Be a sponge for new insights and be open to new ideas. Learn new skills. I've often heard the advice that you should try to learn something every day. If you are alert enough, you can learn something every hour! Each time you learn something, be grateful not only that there is so much *to learn* but that you may be lucky enough to live in a place where you are permitted to learn.

**FEED YOUR SPIRIT.** Of course, meditation and spiritual beliefs are germane, yet there is more you can do:

- Nature is also good for the soul, and it is alive with an energy that is available to you at any time. You don't have to go far to see the sky or hear a bird chirp.
- Art is the food of the soul. You don't need to be a professional artist to benefit from its gifts. The same is true for all the other forms of art.
- Singing is good for the soul. Even if you sing badly, sing from your heart and allow your own sound to burst through. It makes no difference how well you sing—it will benefit you greatly and improve your mental, physical, and spiritual health. And you can do it privately, you don't have to sing in front of anybody.
- Dance, no matter how poor you are at dancing (nobody has to be watching).

- Drawing feeds your spirit and your right brain. It doesn't matter if you think you can draw or not—because, again, this is for *your* benefit, not for the rest of the world. Draw simple mandalas just for the creativity of it.
- Write your thoughts or a story. It is a great opportunity for self-expression and even for creating a new narrative for your life. This is one of the reasons that journaling is so popular and so beneficial.

The more you sing, dance, draw, exercise, write, or engage in any creative activity, the more you will benefit yourself, and thus the more you will be able to benefit others with the new and improved you!

Participating directly in some kind of artistic form of expression will feed your soul as much as meditation and mindfulness. Every little thing you do to honor yourself will make you happier and will benefit others.

## You Can Just *Be*

You do not have to search for activities. There is nothing wrong with passive participation either. There are many beautiful or thought-provoking pieces of art to see, music to listen to, dances to watch, and other forms of art that remind you how amazing humans, as a species, can be.

## In Summary

Find whatever makes your soul sing and enjoy it. Find new things to appreciate, experience, and observe. Focus on taking care of yourself as a daily part of life.

Once you take care of yourself, you can also take care of others, and contribute to the world.

# CHAPTER 28

# How to Be a Beautiful Hero With a Meaningful Life

*"Nothing can dim the light which shines from within."*
*— Maya Angelou*

HEROES COME IN DIFFERENT FORMS. There are the purely fictional heroes we find in comic books and action movies, such as Batman, Wonder Woman, Captain America, Black Panther, or James Bond. Then there are the kinds of heroes we find in real life, like firefighters, emergency service workers, and members of our armed forces.

What do all versions have in common?

A hero is someone who places the lives of others before their own comfort or safety, just like bodhisattvas do! And that's how you can be a hero. Take care of yourself for sure, gather everything that will make you a better person, and then use it for the benefit of others.

To see ourselves as beautiful heroes requires another way of looking at things. Let's look at the words:

**BEAUTIFUL.** What does beautiful even mean and who decides what beauty is? Let's just take the word at face value: Beautiful means full of beauty. Many of us believe that beauty is an external factor—a beautiful face, a beautiful home, or a beautiful piece of jewelry. But real beauty is an inside job. You become full of beauty because there is something inside you that makes you beautiful, such as your spirit, your kindness, or your compassion. Beautiful is never lasting or real if it is only seen from external appearances. When you focus on making yourself a good person, a helpful person, and a pleasant or caring person, you have strong chance of more fully developing the Virtues of the Heart. And the more beautiful you become.

**A MEANINGFUL LIFE.** So many people are drawn to explore ways to have a more meaningful life. They long to live a life of value. Some people truly believe they were put on this earth to achieve a purpose. Many artists, singers, inventors, healers, entertainers, and others with special talents say: "I was born to do this. God gave me a special skill and put me on earth to use it." That may be true for them, and there is no doubt that many people have a great purpose in life that they actively pursue each day.

But let's think about it another way. Some people are still searching for their purpose. They crave a purpose-driven life, but their task is to find out what it is. And, quite frankly, not everyone will find their beautiful, meaningful life by doing something that will land them on the news, leading medical breakthroughs, or marked for greatness in history books.

- If you can cure cancer and save many lives, that's a welcome miracle!
- If you can be a great entertainer and bring happiness to great numbers of people, that's so cool!
- If you can invent something that will make millions of people happy, that's awesome!

But how many of you will find the cure for cancer? How many of you will invent the smart phone, the computer, or consumer travel to the International Space Station? How many of you will become stars in the entertainment world? Statistically, the chances are low.

## The Next Big Thing Isn't Always Better

If you think that major accomplishments are what it takes to have a meaningful life, you will be doomed to a feeling that you never quite match up to others. If most people believe it's important to be nothing less than spectacular and get a round of applause for all we do, then most of us will fall short. The vast majority of humans do not have celebrity status and do not live by those kinds of standards. If we were to believe that the size or significance of our public contributions or personas were what brought meaning to life, then few of us would feel we were leading meaningful lives. We would end up judging ourselves harshly and it would be difficult to find a purpose in following the call of the soul.

Judging what is meaningful against what is successful would preclude too many from a life of meaning.

- What if your talent is that you could be a great pianist? What if you live in a country where your chances of *having* a piano, let alone being able to find a way and the money to train and hone that skill, are virtually non-existent? Then you are powerless to pursue this as a purpose in life.

- What if you were a writer living in a communist country where no one gets to choose what they will pursue. Someone tells you exactly where you will work and what kind of work you will do. If writing professionally was your only way to find purpose, you would feel powerless or it could require living elsewhere to do so. This doesn't mean you can't or won't write, but you would have limited outlets for sharing your work and might have to do it in secret. It could literally be dangerous if it was the only way you could finding meaning.

There are so many ways that the larger goals and dreams in life may not work out or be sustained in all parts of your lifetime. So depending on these things to happen in order to have a meaningful life could rob you of having a meaningful life.

What if we looked at it this way: Instead of life having an inherent meaning or a meaning that is dependent upon some external success, you recognize that life only has the meaning that you find in it or assign to it? In that scenario, you are free, no matter where you live or what kind of oppression or disappointment you face.

## Finding Meaning in Being Kind

The Buddhist monks that I know are highly intelligent and educated but I'm reasonably sure that none of them will ever cure cancer, invent the next "big thing," or become movie stars. I'm even much more certain that none of them would think that their life has no meaning.

As people who have taken the bodhisattva vow, if I were to ask any of them, "What are you here for?" I am pretty certain that each and every one of them, without any hesitation, would answer, "I am here to help everyone else." How profoundly simple! Virtually all that they own is two robes. They are very certainly not rich or what we think of as powerful, yet they are the happiest people I have ever met.

This is how I know that any one of us can tap into our inner beauty and we can all find meaning even in simple acts. You can find purpose in quiet, unpublicized generosity. You can feel the joy of being good, feeling like a good person, and sharing goodness. The monks live from the Four Virtues of the Heart. The more you focus on cultivating the virtues of the heart, the more you will see a kind, compassionate, and joyful life—for everyone!

## It's as Simple as a Smile

All you have to do is smile at everyone you meet and greet them pleasantly and you will make countless people happier and better their day. If you couple that with actually caring about them and doing whatever you can for them, you will positively affect countless people. To me, this is living a meaningful life.

Who doesn't love a friendly person? Who doesn't want to be seen? Who doesn't appreciate kindness, sympathy, and joy? You can have meaning in your life and make the world a better place with little more than a smile, a nod, or a wave.

Generosity is important. Some people give away money, time, or knowledge. Every contribution helps, but it does not mean you will get the same in return. But when you give away love, you will always have more than you started with. It flows back to you a millionfold. The more you give the more your get. Working on cultivating the virtues of the heart constantly replenishes you and enables you to have more love to give.

## Support the Heroes in Our World

We are all heroes. It is time that, together as a nation, we shine our lights as brightly as we can and "pour" more compassion and kindness into our societies, everywhere!

It is our natural way of being, but we must remember to do so with intention. It is our choice. If we choose love and compassion as a way of being every day, we will transform our world.

In America, we often find ourselves polarized. I believe we can get back on track by remembering the Golden Rule. Treat others with respect, even if you disagree. We are human beings and we need to be kind to one another. It is more important to loving than to be right.

## Thank Your Personal Heroes

Part of being a hero is to acknowledge the heroes in your own life and thank them for being amazing role models and for all they have given.

I want to thank all of you who have come on the journey with me.

I want to thank all of those who have helped me in any way.

To all of those who have loved me ...

To all of those who have brought me more happiness...

To all of those who have blessed and enhanced my life physically, materially, emotionally, or spiritually ...

Because of you, I have become more of who I am meant to be. And I have gained the strength, wisdom, and compassion to share what I have learned. I am so filled with love. I am so grateful to be surrounded by beautiful heroes and wisdom teachers. My life is so filled with meaning. Because of this, I have more to offer.

You who are reading and you who have come before as teachers and guides, you are *my* heroes.

**May you be happy.**
**May you be healthy.**
**May you live with ease.**
**May you be free of all the causes that will impede any of those things for you.**

To all of you, and everyone everywhere, I wish you the same.

If you doubt that you can help change the world, let me remind you of a quote by renowned anthropologist Margaret Mead:

*"Never doubt that a small group of thoughtful, committed citizens can change the world; indeed, it's the only thing that ever has."*

Thank you!
Lexie Brockway Potamkin

# We Are All Connected

*"Before you finish eating breakfast,
you've depended on more than half the world."*
— *Martin Luther King Jr.*

The above quote was from a lecture known as "The Christmas Sermon on Peace," delivered in 1967. The idea expressed is not something new. Remember that it was the very basis of the philosophy we discussed in Chapter 18 that described the Great Chain of Being, which is thousands of years old.

Almost every religion and spiritual teaching counsels us to love everyone. Judaism and Christianity teach us, "Thou shalt love thy neighbor as thyself." But kindness, compassion, and caring about others can be found in faiths across the world.

However, you do not have to be religious, or even remotely spiritual, to abide by the notion that we must practice a form of brotherhood and sisterhood that allows us to make sure people of all backgrounds, traditions, and nations are cared for and treated respectfully. We are all connected. And when one person, group, or community suffers we all suffer. When one race of people is oppressed or in harm's way, it impacts us all.

The idea that we are all connected is also a very practical matter and can be found in our secular world of business. In the classic work on economics by Adam Smith, *The Wealth of Nations*, he suggests that every person, even working for their own best interests, finds it advantageous to work with others. Honoring the connection we all have makes wonderful things happen.

Clearly, we have arrived at a moment in human history where we must truly respect the lives and views of others. We must pay attention to any of the ways in which we contribute to making some people feel less important or marginalized. We have to be mindful of our own prejudices and of how our views, words, and actions impact others.

It is crucial that we understand the interconnected nature of our world. And that we honor the notion that in order for us to be happy, others must be happy too.

All human beings deserve respect, human rights, prosperity, a safe place to live, medical care, and that their needs be met. We have to recognize that individuals in marginalized groups suffer greatly. We must seek to correct wrong thinking and any ill feelings we may consciously or unconsciously direct at a particular group. This is where compassion is key.

My work with the International League for Human Rights and with the Tibetan monks for all these years has also taught me the pain of cultures and peoples who are oppressed and killed based on race and religious beliefs. The Chinese government imprisoned and killed so many monks and nuns. They drove so many Tibetan Buddhists from their beloved country. This is why the Dalai Lama lives in exile in Northern India. His homeland was taken. Despite that, he and all Buddhist monks radiate love, compassion, and hope.

My friends and colleagues at the SEE Learning program™ and the Center for Contemplative Science and Compassion-Based Ethics at Emory University put it best: "Through awareness of, connection with, and compassion for ourselves and each other, we can begin to recognize, challenge and transform those aspects of the systems that perpetuate apathy, violence, and injustice."

If people can be taught to hate, they can also be taught to love. May we all give and receive the love we deserve.

♥

## FINAL EXERCISE

# Creating a Life Philosophy
# that Brings You Joy

*"A personal philosophy defines who you are*
*and what you stand for."*
— *Isaac Breese*

I AM SO HONORED THAT YOU have taken the time to read my book. It was very meaningful to me to share my journey.

We each have our own personal road to walk, but I hope that some of what I shared offered insights and information that adds value to your life.

This final exercise is important. It is a chance for you to assess your current life philosophy influences and choose some new ideas to add into the mix.

Remember, part of expanding your Personal Life Philosophy is being able to embrace new ideas and people who may have different points of views and experiences. This requires us to have clarity and awareness of who we are and what shaped us. It also helps to become aware of any prejudices that we may have been raised with, either those that you harbor regarding others or that have been used against you. If you look at the things that you were exposed to in your childhood and growing up years, it will give you a sense of where bias comes from. And admitting to it and naming it is a first step to getting past it.

## 1.  Look at the Facts About Your Life

First, let's take a moment to identify the aspects of your life and upbringing that have helped to formulate your personal philosophy. It helps to just consider where some of your point of view is coming from. These are just facts and not intended to stir any judgement.

Identify the things that have influenced your journey:
- Age and generational influences
- Religious and spiritual orientation
- Ethnic and racial identity
- Socioeconomic status
- Physical or developmental disability
- Disability developed later in life
- National origin
- Indigenous heritage
- Sexual orientation
- Gender or preferred pronouns

## 2.  Consider Cultural Influences in Your Life

Ask yourself these questions about how your culture of origin has influenced you in terms of relating to others from different backgrounds or embracing ideas from other cultures.
- What are some of my learned values and shared attitudes among similar groups of people?
- How has cultural heritage shaped who I am, how I see myself, and how others see me?
- How do these influences affect my comfort level in certain groups?
- What is the relationship between my visible identity and my self-identifications, and how is this influenced by my cultural context of understanding others?
- What kind of assumptions are people likely to make about me based on my visible identity, my sociocultural

context, and what I choose to share about myself?

- How might my areas of privilege affect my understanding of others?

### 3. Review the Questions from the Preface

Now, revisit the questions from the preface of this book. If you haven't already, give them some thought and answer them as best you can:

- What are the greatest influences of my childhood?

- How have my parents guided or influenced my principles?

- How were my grandparents a source of wisdom or insight?

- How did religion, culture, ethnicity or location of birth shape me?

- Was there a personal or family trauma or loss that impacted my views on life?

- Did childhood dreams inspire certain beliefs?

- Who are my role models today, personal and professional?

- What are some of the ethics I believe in?

- What are my core values?

- What are my most important principles?

- What core beliefs rule my life?

- What is my personal philosophy on life?

- What did I believe as a child that I wish I could still believe today?

- What do I wish there was more of in the world?

- What is most important to me?

4. **Try This Writing Exercise**

When you begin to look more deeply at the aspects of upbringing and life that formed your personal philosophy, you may find that awareness will lead to greater happiness.

List those things you love about your upbringing and culture. Things you would like to celebrate and focus on more:

_____

_____

_____

_____

List those things you no longer relate to about your growing up years and your influences. Things you would like to release or reinvent:

_____

_____

_____

_____

Describe how you identify yourself in one paragraph:

_____

_____

_____

_____

My most powerful personal quality:

_____

_____

_____

_____

What I stand for and believe in:

_____

_____

_____

_____

What holds the greatest value to me in life?:

_____

_____

_____

_____

My role models are:

_____

_____

_____

_____

The moral compass that guides me is:

_____

_____

_____

_____

My personal ethics include these beliefs:

_____

_____

_____

_____

Are there certain cultures or practices that appeal to you but that are not part of your upbringing? Are you exploring them, or would you like to? Write them down:

_____

_____

_____

_____

A personal philosophy is a set of guiding principles that we live by. Based on the above answers, write a paragraph or a page about what your personal philosophy on life is:

_____

_____

_____

_____

Now, write a shorter version. This is something you can carry with you or tape to your computer as a reminder:

_____

_____

_____

_____

## 5. Write Statement that Encapsulates Your New Life Philosophy

*For example:*

"I believe that a person's ethics, integrity, and values are an important part of living a healthy and meaningful life. Knowing this, I try to operate from a moral compass within that directs my behavior. Being compassionate and kind, and also, offering my smile to the world, are important aspects of who I am. I love the values imparted to me by my parents and I know they live within me. But I also love that I have the absolute freedom to choose what I believe. I am an embodiment of many different philosophies. I am grateful that I have the self-awareness to seek, learn about, and include aspects of many traditions in my life. I am committed to helping people live their lives with greater purpose by helping them develop self-awareness."

## In Summary

The beautiful thing about your personal philosophy is that it's yours and you can choose to tweak it, add to it, let things go, and explore new ideas at any stage in life. You are never too old. And you are never too young. And even if you come from a life that was strict or guarded as a child, as an adult you can make new choices. Follow your heart. Trust your intuition. And learn, learn, learn as much as you can.

Ralph Waldo Emerson is noted for greeting friends with the question, "What has become clear to you since we last met?" His intent, according to historians, was an invitation to challenge guests to assess the progress of their thinking. There is always room to grow and new ways to know yourself!

*"Being entirely honest with oneself is a good exercise."*
*— Sigmund Freud*

# CHAPTER NOTES

**Front of Book:**
Epigraph: This quote is widely attributed to Ancient Greek Philosopher Aristotle.

**Introduction:** You Have the Power to Know Yourself and Transform Yourself
Epigraph: Adapted for modern times from this quote from psychologist Abraham Maslow: "What is necessary to change a person is to change his awareness of himself," found at www.brainyquote.com/quotes/abraham_maslow_132272.

**Part One: Understanding the Roots of Personal Philosophies and Values**

**Chapter 1:** Embracing People of All Backgrounds
Epigraph one: Robert Alan (1922-1978) was known as an American writer, artist and social activist.

Epigraph two: Sneha Maheswari is author of numerous inspiring quotes on social media who describes herself as a student of English Literature.

**Chapter 2:** How Our Personal Philosophies Develop
Epigraph: Roy T. Bennett is author of *The Light in the Heart*.

Amir-Aeon, Dorsa. "Our environment shapes our personality much more than we
    think." *Fast Company*, 9 Jan. 2020, www.fastcompany.com/90449165/
    our-environment-shapes-our-personality-much-more-than-we-think.
"Early Childhood Trauma." *The National Child Traumatic Stress Network*, www.
    nctsn.org/what-is-child-trauma/trauma-types/early-childhood-trauma.
Hays, Pamela. *Addressing Cultural Complexities in Practice: Assessment,
    Diagnosis, and Therapy, Third Edition*. American Psychological
    Association, 2016.
Mitchell, Travis. "Religion in Everyday Life." *Pew Research Center: Religion
    and Public Life*, 12 Apr. 2016, www.pewforum.org/2016/04/12/religion-
    in-everyday-life.
Thornton, Stephen P. "Sigmund Freud." *Internet Encyclopedia of Philosophy*,
    www.iep.utm.edu/freud.

**Chapter 3:** Where Do Core Values and Principles Come From?
Epigraph: Sunday Adelaja is founder and senior pastor of the Embassy of the Blessed Kingdom of God for All Nations in Kiev, Ukraine.

**Chapter 4:** Why Compassion Is So Important

Epigraph: Rev. Dr. John Watson DD was known for his role as a minister of the Free Church of Scotland, but he also wrote fiction as Maclaren.

Cherry, Kendra. "The Age Old Debate of Nature vs. Nurture." *Verywell Mind*, 3 June 2020, www.verywellmind.com/what-is-nature-versus-nurture-2795392.

**Part Two: Buddhist Philosophy and Practices for Lasting Happiness**

**Chapter 5:** My Calling to Buddhism
Epigraph: The Dalai Lama, often addressed as His Holiness, is the spiritual and political leader of the Tibetan people, currently living in exile in Dharamsala, India. This and many of his epigraphs have been widely circulated; they come from his speaking engagements, books, and many appearances to his followers.

**Chapter 6:** The Buddha Offered an Approach to Life
Epigraph: Dr. *Tapas Kumar Aich* is an India-based Psychiatrist and Professor who sees the value in the Buddha's psychological approach.

Aich, Tapas Kumar. "Buddha philosophy and Western psychology." *Indian Journal of Psychiatry*, vol. 55, suppl. 2, Jan. 2013, pp. S165-S170. *National Center for Biotechnology Information*, doi: 10.4103/0019-5545.105517, www.ncbi.nlm.nih.gov/pmc/articles/PMC3705677.

Bhikkhu, Thanissaro. "What Do Buddhists Mean When They Talk About Emptiness?" *Tricycle: The Buddhist Review*, Spring 1997, tricycle.org/magazine/what-do-buddhists-mean-when-they-talk-about-emptiness.

Geshe Lobsang Tenzin Negi, PhD. *Center for Compassion, Integrity and Secular Ethics*, http://www.compassion.life.edu/team/geshe-lobsang-tenzin-negi-ph-d.

"Life and teachings of the Buddha." *BBC Bitesize*, https://www.bbc.co.uk/bitesize/guides/zd8bcj6/revision/1.

"Noble Eightfold Path." *Wikipedia*, en.wikipedia.org/wiki/Noble_Eightfold_Path.

Rahula, Walpola Sri. "The Noble Eightfold Path." *Tricycle: The Buddhist Review*, https://tricycle.org/magazine/noble-eightfold-path/.

Richmond, Lewis. "Emptiness: The Most Misunderstood Word in Buddhism." *Huffpost*, 6 Mar. 2013, www.huffpost.com/entry/emptiness-most-misunderstood-word-in-buddhism_b_2769189.

"Sangha." *Britannica*, www.britannica.com/topic/sangha.

**Chapter 7:** Embracing the Four Virtues of the Heart — Virtues One and Two
Epigraph: Robert Thurman is an America Buddhist academic and author who has written and translated books on Tibetan Buddhism. He was a Professor of

Indo-Tibetan Buddhist Studies at Columbia University.

**Chapter 8:** Embracing the Four Virtues of the Heart — Virtues Three and Four
Epigraph: Barbara De Angelis is an American author, lecturer and spiritual teacher.

Sources Used in Chapters 7 and 8

Bates, Claire. "Is this the world's happiest man? Brain scans reveal French monk found to have 'abnormally large capacity' for joy - thanks to meditation." *Daily Mail*, 31 Oct. 2012, www.dailymail.co.uk/health/article-2225634/Is-worlds-happiest-man-Brain-scans-reveal-French-monk-abnormally-large-capacity-joy-meditation.html.

Cherry, Kendra. "Phineas Gage's Astonishing Brain Injury." *Verywell Mind*, 2 Apr. 2020, www.verywellmind.com/phineas-gage-2795244.

"Cultivating Cherishing Wisdom: Upekkha Bhavana." *Mindful Yoga*, durhamyoga.wordpress.com/cultivating-cherishing-wisdom-upekkha-bhavana.

O'Brien, Barbara. "Brahma-Vihara: The Four Immeasurable Virtues of Buddhism." *Learn Religions*, 16 Apr. 2019, www.learnreligions.com/brahma-vihara-the-four-divine-states-449717.

O'Brien, Barbara. "The Buddhist Practice of Loving Kindness (Metta)." *ThoughtCo*, 2 Jan. 2020, www.thoughtco.com/loving-kindness-metta-449703.

"The Science of Compassion." *Compassionate Action Network*, www.compassionateactionnetwork.org/science-of-compassion.

Tiret, Holly, "Compassion: Who needs it? We all do!" *Michigan State University*, 17 Mar. 2014, www.canr.msu.edu/news/compassion_who_needs_it_we_all_do.

Tran, Alex. "Brahma-Vihara: The Four Divine States or Four Immeasurables of Buddhism." *Seattle Yoga News*, 8 June 2016, seattleyoganews.com/brahma-vihara-the-four-divine-states-or-four-immeasurables-of-buddhism.

**Chapter 9:** The Jewel in the Lotus and Sacred Symbols
Epigraph: Dōgen (1200-1253), known also as Jōyō Daishi, or Kigen Dōgen, was a leading Japanese Buddhist known for introducing Zen to Japan via the Soto school. The Epigraph comes from, *A Primer Of Soto Zen.*

"Avalokiteshvara." Britannica, www.britannica.com/topic/Avalokiteshvara.

"Avalokiteshvara." Wikipedia, https://en.wikipedia.org/wiki/Avalokite%C5%9Bvara.

Campbell, Charlie. "The Dalai Lama Has Been the Face of Buddhism for 60 Years. China Wants to Change That." Time, 7 Mar. 2019, time.com/longform/dalai-lama-60-year-exile.

Dōgen. *A Primer of Soto Zen: A Translation of Dogen's Shobogenzo Zuimonki.* Translated by Reiho Masunaga, University of Hawaii Press, 1979.

"Guanyin, the Chinese Goddess of Mercy." CITS, www.cits.net/china-travel-guide/guanyin-the-chinese-goddess-of-mercy.html.

"Guan Yin, Guan Yim, Kuan Yim, Kuan Yin." One World Nations Online, www.nationsonline.org/oneworld/Chinese_Customs/Guan_Yin.htm.

"Jana Baha Dyah Jatra." *Wikipedia*, en.wikipedia.org/wiki/Jana_Baha_Dyah_Jatra.

Nielsen, Eric. "What jewel is in the lotus?" Quora, 25 Dec. 2018, www.quora.com/What-jewel-is-in-the-lotus.

Nolan, Josephine. "Guan Yin and the Ten Great Protections of the Goddess of Mercy: Avalokiteshvara, Bodhisattva of Compassion." *Buddha Weekly: Buddhist Practices, Mindfulness, Meditation*, buddhaweekly.com/guan-yin-ten-great-protections-goddess-mercy-avalokiteshvara-bodhisattv.

"Om Mani Padme Hum." *The Joy Within*, 23 Apr. 2019, thejoywithin.org/meditations/mantras/om-mani-padme-hum

"Om Mani Padme Hum." *Wikipedia*, en.wikipedia.org/wiki/Om_mani_padme_hum.

"Sacred Dedication: A Korean Buddhist Masterpiece." *National Museum of Asian Art*, asia.si.edu/exhibition/sacred-dedication-a-korean-buddhist-masterpiece.

Spacey, John. "Kannon: Mysterious Smile of a Japanese Goddess." Japan Talk, 18 May 2014, www.japan-talk.com/jt/new/kannon.

"Tara (Buddhism)." Wikipedia, en.wikipedia.org/wiki/Tara_(Buddhism).

"What Om Mani Padme Hum Means?" *Shambhala Publications*, www.shambhala.com/snowlion_articles/om-mani-padme-hum-dalai-lama.

**Chapter 10:** Tonglen — The Ultimate Exercise
Epigraph: Dhaval Patel is a proponent of personal growth and blogs about it at Zenful Sprit. This Epigraph came from his article, "A Beginners Guide to Tonglen Meditation."

Bhikkhu, Thanissaro. "The Buddha's Original Teachings on Mindfulness." *Tricycle: The Buddhist Review*, 5 Mar. 2018, tricycle.org/trikedaily/satipatthana-sutta-mindfulness.

Chodron, Pema. "How to Practice Tonglen." *Lion's Roar*, 20 May, 2020, www.lionsroar.com/how-to-practice-tonglen.

Patel, Dhaval. "The Beginner's Guide to Tonglen Meditation." *Zenful Spirit*, 28 Mar. 2017, zenfulspirit.com/2017/03/28/beginners-guide-tonglen-meditation.

"The Three Vehicles." *Soka Gakkai Nichiren Buddhism Library*, www.nichirenlibrary.org/en/dic/Content/T/190.

**Chapter 11:** The Buddhist Approach to Happiness

Epigraph one: Epictetus was a Greek Stoic philosopher known to have a religious tone and attracted early Christian thinkers. In this epigraph on happiness, he exercises good old common sense.

Epigraph two: Eric Hoffer was known as a social philosopher who wrote many books, including *The Ordeal of Change* (1963). He was awarded the Presidential Medal of Freedom in February 1983.

Bloom, Linda and Charlie Bloom. "Research Proves Money Can't Buy Happiness." *Psychology Today*, 5 May 2015, www.psychologytoday. com/us/blog/stronger-the-broken-places/201505/research-proves-money-cant-buy-happiness.

Brown, Joshua and Joel Wong. "How Gratitude Changes You and Your Brain." *Greater Good Magazine*, 6 Jun. 2017, greatergood.berkeley.edu/article/ item/how_gratitude_changes_you_and_your_brain.

"Giving thanks can make you happier." *Harvard Health Publishing*, www.health. harvard.edu/healthbeat/giving-thanks-can-make-you-happier.

MacMillan, Amanda. "Money Can't Buy Happiness, But It Does Change How You Experience It." *Time*, 19 Dec. 2017, https://time.com/5071079/ happiness-income.

Novotney, Amy. "Money Can't Buy Happiness." *Monitor on Psychology*, vol. 23, no. 7, 2012, www.apa.org/monitor/2012/07-08/money.

Quoidbach, Jordi, et. al. "Money Giveth, Money Taketh Away." *Psychological Science*, vol. 21, no. 6, 18 May 2010, pp. 759-763. *Sage Journals*, journals.sagepub.com/doi/abs/10.1177/0956797610371963.

Steig, Cory. "How you think about money can impact how happy you are in life, study says." *CNBC Make It*, 5 Sep. 2019, https://www.cnbc. com/2019/09/05/can-money-buy-happiness-debate-study-on-success.html.

Wong, Y. Joel, et. al. "Does gratitude writing improve the mental health of psychotherapy clients? Evidence from a randomized controlled trial." *Psychotherapy Research*, vol. 28, no. 2, 3 May 2016, pp. 192-202. *Taylor & Francis Online*, www.tandfonline.com/doi/full/10.1080/10503 307.2016.1169332.

**Chapter 12:** The Value of Struggle

Epigraph: Friedrich Nietzsche (1844-1900) was a German classical scholar, philosopher, and critic of culture who became a very influential modern thinker. The epigraph comes from his book, *Twilight of the Idols* (1888), which when translated means: *"What does not kill me makes me stronger."* The essence of the epigraph may have been made popular in the movie, "Steel Magnolias."

Baer, Drake. "New Study Destroys Malcolm Gladwell's 10,000 Hour Rule." *Business Insider*, 3 Jul. 2014, www.businessinsider.com/new-study-destroys-malcolm-gladwells-10000-rule-2014-7.

"List of emotions." *Wikipedia*, simple.wikipedia.org/wiki/List_of_emotions.

**Chapter 13:** Suffering and Loss
Epigraph: The Buddha said many wise things over 2,500 years ago and yet many, like this epigraph, stand up to time. He helped people understand the source of their pain and gave them tools to heal it. The Buddhist approach to alleviating suffering continues as an enduring way to cope with life and hardships.

"Buddhism: An Introduction." *PBS*, www.pbs.org/edens/thailand/buddhism.htm.

Littlefair, Sam. "What is Suffering?" *Lion's Roar*, 30 Apr. 2020, www.lionsroar.com/what-is-suffering-10-buddhist-teachers-weigh-in.

**Chapter 14:** Buddhism and Self-Esteem
Epigraph one: The Buddha also taught that we deserve happiness, which makes this epigraph so stunning when it comes to Self-love.

Epigraph two: The author's mother had a plaque with this Helen Steiner Rice epigraph: "Love works in ways that are wonderful and strange. There is nothing in life that love cannot change." It is adapted from a larger work by Helen Steiner Rice (1900-1981), who was a beloved American writer of inspirational and religious poetry. She wrote books and was known for her epigraphs and poems on greeting cards. Full text of that poem can be found at: www.goodreads.com/Epigraphs/7521185-love-is-like-magic-and-it-always-will-be-for.

**Chapter 15:** Buddhism and Science
Epigraph: The Buddha, founder of Buddhism, spoke those words unfamiliar to foreigners. The epigraph used to start this chapter is a version that has been translated more appropriately for Western readers. For your reference, here is the original as it appears in the *Kalama Sutta:*

"Do not go upon what has been acquired by repeated hearing; nor upon tradition; nor upon rumor; nor upon what is in a scripture; nor upon surmise; nor upon an axiom; nor upon specious reasoning; nor upon a bias towards a notion that has been pondered over; nor upon another's seeming ability; nor upon the consideration, 'The monk is our teacher.' Rather, when you yourselves know that these things are good; these things are not blamable; undertaken and observed, these things lead to benefit and happiness, then and only then enter into and abide in them."— The Buddha

This chapter was inspired by His Holiness The Dalia Lama's, passion for science. For the purpose of gathering precise insights from His Holiness this chapter refers often to the beautiful documentary: Dalai Lama, Scientist - which can be downloaded for view at the Peacejam Foundation website: www.peacejam.org/the-dalai-lama-scientist.

Abrahams, Matthew. "Buddhism Is What Science Should Be Doing." *Tricycle: The Buddhist Review*, 21 Jun. 2019, tricycle.org/trikedaily/buddhist-science.

Barash, David. "Is Buddhism the Most Science-Friendly Religion?" *Scientific American*, 11 Feb. 2014, blogs.scientificamerican.com/guest-blog/is-buddhism-the-most-science-friendly-religion.

Bodhi, Bhikkhu, ed. *In the Buddha's Words: An Anthology of Discourses from the Pāli Canon. Wisdom Publications*, 2015.

"Buddhism and Science." *Wikipedia*, en.wikipedia.org/wiki/Buddhism_and_science.

Clarke, Cath. "The Dalai Lama: Scientist review - a mildly enlightening soft-focus insight." *The Guardian*, 21 May 2020, www.theguardian.com/film/2020/may/21/the-dalai-lama-scientist-review.

"Dialogue between Modern Science and Buddhist Science." *His Holiness the 14th Dalai Lama of Tibet*, 16 Nov. 2018, www.dalailama.com/news/2018/dialogue-between-modern-science-and-buddhist-science.

"Dialogue between Modern Science and Buddhist Science." *YouTube*, uploaded by His Holiness the 14th Dalai Lama of Tibet, 17 Nov. 2018, www.youtube.com/watch?v=YLFb5vHeBJU.

Dunne, John. "Is Buddhism Scientific or Religious?" *Tricycle: The Buddhist Review*, 7 Jan. 2019, tricycle.org/trikedaily/buddhism-scientific-religious.

Frank, Adam. "Buddhism, Science, and the Western World." *Cosmos and Culture*, 11 May 2017, www.npr.org/sections/13.7/2017/05/11/527533776/buddhism-and-science.

Gross, Terry. "The Lost Art of Breathing Can Impact Sleep and Resilience." *NPR*, 27 May 2020, https://www.npr.org/sections/health-shots/2020/05/27/862963172/how-the-lost-art-of-breathing-can-impact-sleep-and-resilience.

Gyatso, Tenzin. "Science at the Crossroads." *His Holiness the 14th Dalai Lama of Tibet*, 2005, www.dalailama.com/messages/buddhism/science-at-the-crossroads.

Hauck, Carley. "How People Learn to Increase Their Resilience." *Mindful*, 3 Mar. 2016, www.mindful.org/how-people-learn-to-increase-their-resilience.

Lopez, Donald. "The Scientific Buddha: Past, Present, Future – 'A Purified Religion.'" *YouTube*, uploaded by Yale University, 11 Dec. 2014, www.youtube.com/watch?v=10BdHm7E6cM.

Lopez Jr., Donald S. "The Scientific Buddha." *Tricycle: The Buddhist Review*, Winter 2012, tricycle.org/magazine/scientific-buddha.

Samuel, Geoffrey Brian. "Between Buddhism and Science, Between Mind and Body." *Religions*, vol. 5, no. 3, Sep. 2014, pp. 560-579. *ResearchGate*, doi:10.3390/rel5030560, www.researchgate.net/publication/272659921_Between_Buddhism_and_Science_Between_Mind_and_Body.

Schedneck, Brooke. "How the Dalai Lama is chosen and why China wants to appoint its own." *The Conversation*, theconversation.com/how-the-dalai-lama-is-chosen-and-why-china-wants-to-appoint-its-own-114351.

Sloan, Jason. "Science in Buddhism." *Encyclopedia of Sciences and Religions*, 2013, https://link.springer.com/referenceworkentry/10.1007%2F978-1-4020-8265-8_886.

Varela, Francisco. "Buddhism and Modern Science." *Mind & Life Institute*, 1 Jul. 2010, www.mindandlife.org/buddhism-modern-science.

Wangchuk, Tashi. "The Dalai Lama-Scientist- A review." *Tibetan Review*, 27 Dec. 2019, www.tibetanreview.net/the-dalai-lama-scientist-a-review.

**Part Three: Adding New Philosophies to Life**

**Chapter 16:** Expanding Your Wisdom Tool Kit
Epigraph: Socrates is considered a father of Western philosophy. He was one of the original Greek philosophers from Athens who brought morality to Western ethical tradition of thought. Today his epigraphs, which are widely shared, continue to inspire us and make us think.

McMullin, Rachel. *History of World Religions: Western Religions. West Chester University Libraries*, library.wcupa.edu/c.php?g=61498&p=395609.

Puett, Michael, and Christine Gross-Loh. *The Path: What Chinese Philosophers Can Teach Us About the Good Life*. Simon & Schuster, 2017.

**Chapter 17**: The Philosophies of Pluralism and Relativism
Epigraph one: Rasheed Ogunlaru is an acclaimed life and business coach known for his motivational style.

Epigraph two: Syed Sharukh is a wisdom teacher and medical intuitive,

Baghramian, Maria, and J. Adam Carter. "Relativism." *The Stanford Encyclopedia of Philosophy*, 2019, https://plato.stanford.edu/archives/

win2019/entries/relativism/.

Desmond-Harris, Jenée. "What exactly is a microaggression?" *Vox*, 16 Feb. 2015, www.vox.com/2015/2/16/8031073/what-are-microaggressions.

"Dualism." *The Basics of Philosophy*, www.philosophybasics.com/branch_ dualism.html.

"Pluralism." *Merriam-Webster*, www.merriam-webster.com/dictionary/pluralism.

"Pluralism and Monism." *Britannica*, www.britannica.com/topic/pluralism-philosophy.

Schaffer, Jonathan. "Monism." *The Stanford Encyclopedia of Philosophy*, 2018, plato.stanford.edu/archives/win2018/entries/monism.

**Chapter 18**: Greek Philosophy
Epigraph: Alexander the Great was an ancient Greek kind of Macedon. The young king was a conqueror but also credited with pithy sayings, like the epigraph in this chapter. He is also known for his wise approach to solving the Gordian knot.

Antia, Meher. "Molecules Inside a Nucleus." *Physics*, physics.aps.org/story/v3/st10.

"Arthur Koestler." *Wikipedia*, en.wikipedia.org/wiki/Arthur_Koestler.

Boje, David. "Holon and Transorganizational Theory." web.nmsu.edu/~dboje/ TDholons.html .

"The Great Chain of Being." *BBC Bitesize,* www.bbc.co.uk/bitesize/guides/ zmjnb9q/revision/2.

"Great Chain of Being" *Britannica*, www.britannica.com/topic/Great-Chain-of-Being.

"The Holon." *Holon*, https://www.holon.se/folke/kurs/Distans/Ekofys/Recirk/ Eng/holarchy_en.shtml.

"Holon (philosophy)." *Wikipedia*, en.wikipedia.org/wiki/Holon_(philosophy).

"Holons: Turtles All the Way Up, Turtles All the Way Down." *YouTube*, uploaded by Integral Life, 11 Oct. 2014, https://www.youtube.com/ watch?v=KJ4UjAFHCGA.

Koestler, Arthur. *The Ghost in the Machine. Hutchinson*, 1967.

Tim. "Socrates: Know Yourself." *The-Philosophy*, 24 Mar. 2012, www.the-philosophy.com/socrates-know-yourself.

"Turtles all the way down." *Wikipedia*, https://en.wikipedia.org/wiki/Turtles_all_ the_way_down.

Velikovsky, JT. "The Holon-Parton Structure of the Meme – A Structure for the Unit of Culture (and also – the Narreme, or `Unit of Narrative', or `Unit of Story')." *StoryAlity Theory*, 12 Dec. 2013, storyality.wordpress. com/2013/12/12/storyality-100-the-holonic-structure-of-the-meme-the-unit-of-culture.

Violatti, Cristian. "Greek Philosophy." *Ancient History Encyclopedia*, 11 Jun. 2013, www.ancient.eu/Greek_Philosophy.

Wilber, Ken. *The Integral Vision: A Very Short Introduction to the Revolutionary Integral Approach to Life, God, the Universe, and Everything*. Shambhala, 2007.

**Chapter 19:** Hindu Philosophy

Epigraph: Dadi Janki was the spiritual leader of the Brahma Kumaris and a friend of the author. She was known for her wise, soulful, and inspiring approach to life and lived until she was 104-years-old.

Alexander, Deepa. "Jiddu Krishnamurti's life - an unusual portrayal." *The Hindu*, 3 Feb. 2020, www.thehindu.com/entertainment/art/jiddu-krishnamurtis-life-through-an-unusual-exhibition/article30726280.ece.

*America Meditates*. 2019, americameditates.org. The official website for *America Meditates*, an event that features music, meditation, yoga and speakers. Founded by Sister Jenna of the Brahma Kumaris.

Audi, Robert. "The Sources of Knowledge." *The Oxford Handbook of Epistemology*, Sep. 2009, www.oxfordhandbooks.com/view/10.1093/oxfordhb/9780195301700.001.0001/oxfordhb-9780195301700-e-3.

"Ayurveda: A Brief Introduction and Guide." *The Ayurvedic Institute*, www.ayurveda.com/resources/articles/ayurveda-a-brief-introduction-and-guide.

Burdick, Gwen. "Sankhya Philosophy." *The Yoga Sanctuary*, www.theyogasanctuary.biz/sankhya-philosophy.

"Dadi Janki, Head of the Brahma Kumaris worldwide religious movement run by women – obituary." *The Telegraph*, 28 Apr. 2020, www.telegraph.co.uk/obituaries/2020/04/28/dadi-janki-head-brahma-kumaris-worldwide-religious-movement.

Ganeri, Jonardon. "Analytic Philosophy in Early Modern India." *The Stanford Encyclopedia of Philosophy*, 2019, plato.stanford.edu/archives/sum2019/entries/early-modern-india.

Guha, Amala. "What is the Philosophy of Ayurvedic Medicine?" *University of Minnesota*, www.takingcharge.csh.umn.edu/what-philosophy-ayurvedic-medicine.

"Hindupedia." *Hindupedia, the Hindu Encyclopedia*, hindupedia.com/en/Main_Page.

"Indian philosophy." *Britannica*, www.britannica.com/topic/Indian-philosophy.

"Meditation Museum." *Brahma Kumaris Meditation Museum*, www.meditationmuseum.org.

Phillips, Stephen. "Epistemology in Classical Indian Philosophy." *The Stanford*

*Encyclopedia of Philosophy*, 2019. plato.stanford.edu/archives/spr2019/
    entries/epistemology-india/.
"Sri Aurobindo." *Sri Aurobindo Ashram*, www.sriaurobindoashram.org/
    sriaurobindo.
"Swami Vishwananda Saraswati." *Yogapedia*, www.yogapedia.com/
    definition/10845/swami-vishwananda-saraswati.
"The Three Sources." *Vedanta Student*, vedantastudent.weebly.com/the-three-
    sources-prasthanatrayi.html.
"Virtuescope." *Brahma Kumaris*, 2020, www.brahmakumaris.org/discovery/
    virtuescope.
What is Vedanta?" *Vedanta Society of Southern California*, vedanta.org/what-is-
    vedanta.
Castillo, Valeria, and Lesson Nine GmbH. "Which Languages Are Spoken In
    India?" *Babbel Magazine*, 15 February, 2015. https://www.babbel.com/
    en/magazine/what-languages-are-spoken-in-india.

**Chapter 20:** Taoist Philosophy
Epigraph: The Tao Te Ching is a Chinese classic authored by the 6th-century
BC sage Laozi, who is widely credited by many as founder of the philosophical
system of Taoism.

Baumard, Nicolas, Hyafil, Alexandre and Boyer, Pascal. "What changed during
    the axial age: Cognitive styles or reward systems?" *Communicative and
    Integrative Biology*, vol. 8, no. 5, 25 Sep. 2015. *NCBI*, doi:10.1080/1942
    0889.2015.1046657.
Cartwright, Mark. "Yin and Yang." *Ancient History Encyclopedia*, 16 May 2018,
    www.ancient.eu/Yin_and_Yang.
Chao-Fong, Léonie. "The 13 Dynasties that Ruled China in Order." *History Hit*,
    10 Jan. 2020, www.historyhit.com/the-dynasties-that-ruled-china-in-order.
"Chinese Revolution." *Britannica*, www.britannica.com/event/Chinese-
    Revolution-1911-1912.
"The Chinese Revolution of 1949." *Office of the Historian*, history.state.gov/
    milestones/1945-1952/chinese-rev.
Mallam, Sally. "Axial Age Thought: Spiritual Foundations of Today." *The Human
    Journey*, humanjourney.us/ideas-that-shaped-our-modern-world-section/
    axial-age-thought-spiritual-foundations-of-today.
Stefon, Matt. "The Axial Age: 5 Fast Facts." *Britannica*, britannica.com/list/the-
    axial-age-5-fast-facts.
"Taoist Philosophy." *Wikipedia*, en.wikipedia.org/wiki/Taoist_philosophy.
"Tao Te Ching – Verse 29." *Hari Nam Singh Healing Heart Center*, www.

harinam.com/tao-te-ching-verse-29-do-you-want-to-improve-the-world-i-dont-think-it-can-be-done.

## Part Four: Meditations and Exercises

**Chapter 21:** Let's Start with Relaxation
Epigraph: The Mayo Clinic is a respected American nonprofit academic medical center. They are focused on integrated patient care, education, and research. They are known for their expertise and their extensive body of content related to every health condition under the sun. Their website is the source of this epigraph.

"Relaxation techniques: Try these steps to reduce stress." *Mayo Clinic*, 18 Apr.
    2020, www.mayoclinic.org/healthy-lifestyle/stress-management/in-depth/relaxation-technique/art-20045368.

**Chapter 22:** How to Meditate
Epigraph: Ajahn Brahm is a British-Australian Theravada Buddhist monk who has written many inspiring books on Buddhism, spirituality, and life. This epigraph is from one of his vast works.

**Chapter 23:** Reflecting on the Endless Knot Exercise
Epigraph: Daisaku Ikeda is a Japanese Buddhist philosopher, educator, and author of many books. This quote appears in "Extreme Poverty: The Gravest Violation of Human Rights" (*The Japan Times*, Dec. 14, 2006), and was reprinted on his website: www.daisakuikeda.org/sub/resources/works/essays/op-eds/jt-oped08.html.

Bryson, Bill. *A Short History of Nearly Everything. Broadway Books*, 2004.
Caron, Matt. "The Endless Knot of Buddhism." *Sivana East*, blog.sivanaspirit.
    com/endless-knot-buddhism.

**Chapter 24:** Walk In Someone Else's Shoes Meditation

Epigraph: Marcus Aurelius was a known as a "stoic philosopher" and was the Roman emperor for a period of time. This epigraph is from *Meditations: A New Translation*, which was published by *Modern Library* in 2003.

"11 Facts About Global Poverty." *Do Something*, www.dosomething.org/us/
    facts/11-facts-about-global-poverty.

**Chapter 25:** Metta Meditation
Epigraph: Amy Leigh Mercree is a medical intuitive and author of bestselling

spirituality books. This epigraph appears in her book, *A Little Bit of Meditation: An Introduction to Mindfulness.*

The Metta Meditation is one of the most important Buddhist exercises for compassion for self and others. The author has participated in and led people through this countless times. This is her explanation and interpretation, and there is not one source for attribution (other than the Buddha, of course).

**Chapter 26:** Wave Exercise
Epigraph: Jalāl ad-Dīn Muhammad Rūmī was a Sufi mystic as well as an Islamic scholar and theologian. This 13th-century Persian poet was also known as Rumi. His works have been translated and quoted widely.

**Part Five: Putting it All Together**

**Chapter 27:** Feed Your Body, Mind, and Spirit
Epigraph: Dee Waldeck runs the Positive Inspirations community on Facebook and elsewhere, offering encouragement to all. Dee's inspirational messages are widely quoted on the internet.

**Chapter 28:** How to Be a Beautiful Hero With a Meaningful Life
Epigraph: Maya Angelou was honored for her work as an American poet, memoirist, and civil rights activist, but she was also seen as a wise woman. Her wisdom was distilled from her published works and her inspiring speaking engagements.

**Afterward:** We Are All Connected
Epigraph: Dr. Martin Luther King, Jr., beloved and heroic civil rights leader and minister, spoke these words during his speech, "A Christmas Sermon on Peace," on December 24, 1967 at the Ebenezer Baptist Church Atlanta, Georgia. The full statement that has been credited to Dr. King is: *"Did you ever stop to think that you can't leave for your job in the morning without being dependent on most of the world? You go to the bathroom and reach for the sponge, and that's handed to you by a Pacific islander. You go into the kitchen to drink your coffee, and that's poured into your cup by a South American. Or maybe you're desirous of having cocoa, and that's poured by a West African. And then you reach over for your toast, and that's given to you at the hands of an English-speaking farmer. Before you finish eating breakfast, you've depended on more than half the world. We aren't going to have peace on Earth until we recognize this basic fact."*

**Final Exercise:** Creating a Life Philosophy that Brings You Joy
Epigraph: Isaac Breese is an aspiring fashion designer who writes about

Christianity, education, and style for *Medium.com*. This quote was taken from Breese's article on personal philosophy.

*https://medium.com/be-unique/the-importance-of-a-personal-philosophy-how-to-create-one-4d281412dbc3*

*Cultural Self-Assessment Survey,* adapted *from Addressing Cultural Complexities in Counseling, can help you begin to look at some of the top influences that have shaped your personal philosophy.*

Final Epigraph: Sigmund Freud is considered the Father of Psychology. This quote appeared in
Masson, J.M. (1985) (Ed.) *The Complete Letters of Sigmund Freud to Wilhelm Fliess, 1887-1904. Cambridge: Harvard University Press*

**From The Author – End Page**
This quote from Ralph Waldo Emmerson is quoted widely and appears in the book *Engaging Worlds*, edited by Robert D. Anderson, Molly Brigid Flynn, and J. Scott Lee.

# KNOW YOURSELF
# Bibliography
## Sources for General Research and Insights

I have read so many books on Buddhist thought and philosophy, as well as other philosophies, that it is difficult to pinpoint the exact source of every bit of knowledge I have acquired over time. So I would like to include the books specifically used for research purposes for *Know Yourself*, along with other books that have inspired me. I hope this will serve to attribute the sources used in the book while also acting as a suggested reading list.

## Buddhism

Chodron, Pema. *The Compassion Book: Teachings for Awakening the Heart.* Shambala, 2017.

Dorje, Ogyen Trinley. *The Heart Is Noble: Changing the World from the Inside Out.* Shambala, 2013.

Feldman, Christina. *Boundless Heart: The Buddha's Path of Kindness, Compassion, Joy, and Equanimity.* Shambala, 2017.

Feldman, Christina. *Compassion: Listening to the Cries of the World.* Shambala, 2003.

Fischer, Norman. *Training in Compassion: Zen Teachings on the Practice of Lojong.* Shambala, 2013.

Fronsdal, Gil. *The Dhammapada: A New Translation of the Buddhist Classic with Annotations.* Shambhala, 2008.

Hagen, Steve. *Buddhism Plain and Simple: The Practice of Being Aware, Right Now, Every Day.* Tuttle Publishing, 2018.

Ladner, Lorne. *The Lost Art of Compassion: Discovering the Practice of Happiness in the Meeting of Buddhism and Psychology.* HarperOne, 2004.

Levine, Stephen. *Becoming Kuan Yin: The Evolution of Compassion.* Weiser Books, 2013.

Powers, John. *A Concise Introduction to Tibetan Buddhism.* Snow Lion, 2008.

Ricard, Matthieu. *Altruism: The Power of Compassion to Change Yourself and the World.* Back Bay Books, 2016.

Rimpoche, Tsem. *Compassion Conquers All: Teachings on the Eight Verses of Mind Transformation.* Weiser, 2014.

Rinpoche, Bokar. *Taking the Bodhisattva Vow.* Trans. Christiane Buchet. Clearpoint Press, 1998.

Shantideva. *A Guide To The Bodhisattva's Way Of Life.* Trans. Vesna Wallace and
     B. Alan Wallace. Snow Lion, 1997.
Siderits, Mark. *Buddhism As Philosophy.* Hackett Publishing Company, 2007.
Townsend, Dominique. *Shantideva: How to Wake Up a Hero.* Wisdom
     Publications, 2015.
Trungpa, Chogyam. *Training the Mind and Cultivating Loving Kindness.*
     Shambala, 2003.
Tuffley, David. *Bodhicaryavatara: A Guide To The Bodhisattva Way Of Life.*
     Altiora Publications, 2011.
Yun, Hsing. *Being Good: Buddhist Ethics for Everyday Life.* Buddha Light Art
     and Living, 2009.

## The Dalai Lama

Bodhi, Bhikkhu. *In the Buddha's Words: An Anthology of Discourses from the
     Pāli Canon.* Wisdom Publications, 2015.
Chodron, Thubten. *Cultivating a Compassionate Heart: Yoga Method of
     Chenrezig.* Snow Lion, 2006.
Dalai Lama. *The Art of Happiness: A Handbook for Living.* Riverhead Books 2009.
Dalai Lama. *Beyond Religion: Ethics for a Whole New World.* Mariner, 2012.
Dalai Lama. *Ethics for a New Millennium.* Riverhead, 2001.
Dalai Lama. *An Open Heart: Practicing Compassion in Everyday Life.* Back Bay
     Books, 2002.
Dalai Lama. *The Wisdom of Compassion: Stories of Remarkable Encounters and
     Timeless Insights.* Riverhead, 2012.
Dalai Lama and Desmond Tutu. *The Book of Joy: Lasting Happiness in a
     Changing World.* Avery, 2016.
Norman, Alexander. *The Dalai Lama: An Extraordinary Life.* Houghton Mifflin
     Harcourt, 2020.

## Greek Philosophy

Broad, William J. *The Oracle: Ancient Delphi and the Science Behind the Lost
     Secrets.* Penguin, 2007.
Scott, Michael. *Delphi: A History of the Center of the Ancient World.* Princeton
     University Press, 2016.

## Holons

Koestler, Arthur. *The Ghost in the Machine.* Hutchinson, 1967.
Wilber, Ken. *The Integral Vision: A Very Short Introduction to the Revolutionary*

*Integral Approach to Life, God, the Universe, and Everything.*
Shambhala, 2007.

## Hinduism

Daniélou, Alain. *The Myths and Gods of India.* Inner Traditions, 1991.
Daniélou, Alain. *Virtue, Success, Pleasure, and Liberation: The Four Aims of Life in the Tradition of Ancient India.* Inner Traditions, 1993.
Feuerstein, Georg. *The Shambhala Encyclopedia of Yoga.* Shambhala, 2000.
Gabriel, Theodore, and Ronald Geaves. *Isms: Understanding Religion.* Universe, 2007.
Kanitkar, V.P., and W. Owen Cole. *Teach Yourself Hinduism: An Introduction.* McGraw-Hill, 2011.
Shapiro, Rami. *The World Wisdom Bible: A New Testament for Global Spirituality.* Skylight Paths, 2017.
Van de Weyer, Robert. *366 Readings from Hinduism.* Pilgrim Press, 2000.

## Neuroscience

Goleman, Daniel, and Richard Davidson. *Altered Traits: Science Reveals How Meditation Changes Your Mind, Brain, and Body.* Avery, 2018.
Kumar, Jay. *Science of A Happy Brain: Thriving in the Age of Anger, Anxiety, and Addiction.* Page Publishing, 2019.
Linden, David J. *Think Tank: Forty Neuroscientists Explore the Biological Roots of Human Experience.* Yale University Press, 2018.

## Philosophy

Allen, James. *As a Man Thinketh.* Penguin, 2009.
Brockway, George M. *Some Thoughts on the Big Questions.* Author House, 2009.
Buckingham, Will, et. al. *The Philosophy Book: Big Ideas Simply Explained.* Dorling Kindersley, 2010.
Puett, Michael, and Christine Gross-Loh. *The Path: What Chinese Philosophers Can Teach Us About the Good Life.* Simon & Schuster, 2017.

## Taoism

Lin, Derek. *Tao Te Ching: Annotated & Explained.* Skylight Paths Publishing, 2006.

## Values, Beliefs, and Relationships

Demartini, John. *The Values Factor: The Secret of Creating an Inspired and*

*Fulfilling Life.*
Berkley Books, 2013.

Dezelic, Marie, and Ghanoum, Gabriel. *Transforming Relationships: Essentials For Building Bridges of Connection.* Presence Press International, 2018.

Haidt, Jonathan. *The Happiness Hypothesis: Finding Modern Truth in Ancient Wisdom.* Basic Books, 2006.

Hays, Pamela A. *Addressing Cultural Complexities in Practice: Assessment, Diagnosis, and Therapy.* American Psychological Association, 2016.

Jampolsky, Gerald G. *Love is Letting Go of Fear.* Celestial Arts, 2010.

Katie, Byron. *Who Would You Be Without Your Story?* Hay House, 2008.

Schelske, Marc Alan. *Discovering Your Authentic Core Values: A Step-by-Step Guide.* Live210  Media, 2012.

## ABOUT THE AUTHOR

Lexie Brockway Potamkin has devoted many years to helping others through her work as a minister, human rights proponent, speaker, and author of many inspirational books. She's met with spiritual leaders across the globe and has studied religion, culture, spirituality, and what makes people happy for over twenty years. Her interest in human nature led her to interview 750 people about life's profound questions for her five-book series, "Messages from the Heart." It was her lifetime study of principles and philosophies from around the world that led her to write Know Yourself.

Lexie had a prominent career in entertainment and business prior to turning her time and talent towards spiritual pursuits and service. A former Miss World USA, she hosted her own talk show and eventually became a public relations professional working for several leading companies. At the height of her business success, having founded and sold her own PR firm, she returned to school for her Master's Degree in Applied Psychology from the University of Santa Monica. Her ensuing counseling work inspired her to the next spiritual step, becoming an ordained minister. She also studied at The Spiritual Paths Institute, a course of study with respected teachers and contemplative wisdom and applied spirituality that combines intellect, heart, and spiritual practice.

She has traveled the globe, exploring many cultures and learning new traditions. Over the past two decades she has been a guiding force and inspiration for many charitable organizations. In Philadelphia, she was President of Resources for Children's Health and a trustee for the International House. Her passion for human rights has led her to speak before the United Nations as Vice President of the International League for Human Rights, and also to work with Tibetan Buddhist monks. She has been a long-time supporter of the work of His Holiness the Dalai Lama and has joyously hosted many spiritual events with monks in his order—from the Drepung Loseling Monastery—as well as participating in related programs here and abroad.

OTHER BOOKS BY LEXIE BROCKWAY POTAMKIN
What is Spirit?
What is Peace?
What is Love?
What is Death?
What is Laughter?
Visit Lexie at: spiritpeacelove.com

# PHOTO ALBUM CAPTIONS

### PHOTO 1
Lexie with Sister Dr. Jenna, who is a spiritual mentor, author, radio, and television personality. She is host of the America Meditating_Radio Show and founder of the Brahma Kumaris Meditation Museum.

### PHOTO 2
Lexie with His Holiness the 14th Dalai Lama.

### PHOTOS 3
Lexie with Dadi Janki, who was the Head of Brahma Kumaris World Spiritual University and founder of Janki Foundation for Spirituality in Healthcare.

### PHOTO 4, 5, 6, 7, 11
Lexie through the years with Monks from The Drepung Loseling Monastery.

### PHOTO 8
Lexie with His Eminence The 102nd Gaden Tripa Kyabje Rizong Sras Rinpoche. The Gaden Tripa position is the highest spiritual position in the Gelug Lineage of Tibetan Buddhism.

### PHOTO 9
Lexie with Geshe Lobsang Tenzin Negi, PhD, His Eminence Sras Rinpoche, and Irene Lee.

### PHOTO 10
Lexie with Kyabje Denma Locho Rinpoche, who was the Tibetan recognized incarnate lama of the Loseling College of Drepung Monastery.

Made in the USA
Coppell, TX
03 December 2020